D1593951

Four Contemporary Korean Plays

Lee Yun-Taek

Translated by Dongwook Kim and Richard Nichols,
with introductions by Richard Nichols

UNIVERSITY PRESS OF AMERICA,® INC.
Lanham • Boulder • New York • Toronto • Plymouth, UK

Copyright © 2007 by
University Press of America,® Inc.
4501 Forbes Boulevard
Suite 200
Lanham, Maryland 20706
UPA Acquisitions Department (301) 459-3366

Estover Road
Plymouth PL6 7PY
United Kingdom

Library of Congress Control Number: 2007924984
ISBN-13: 978-0-7618-3703-9 (paperback : alk. paper)
ISBN-10: 0-7618-3703-5 (paperback : alk. paper)

Contents

Mask of Fire

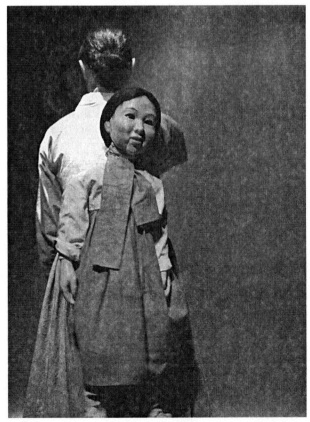

The Dummy Bride

The Dummy Bride

O-Gu

O-Gu

Citizen K

Citizen K

Preface

While there are many translations of modern Korean novels, short stories and poetry, and Korean playwrights' works have been translated into any number of European languages, modern Korean dramatic literature has received but scant attention from English-language translators and, with the exception of *The Wedding Day and Other Korean Plays* (1983), *The Metacultural Theatre of Oh T'ae-Sŏk* (1999), and *Three Plays by Yoo Chi-Jin* (2005), the works translated appear largely in scholarly journals and disparate Web sites. Fortunately, English-language translations of plays by a number of modern Korean playwrights now are in process and should appear in print within a few years.

It may seem strange to some that we chose to translate early works by Lee Yun-Taek; after all, few familiar with Korean theatre would argue that he is Korea's greatest living playwright. (Two leading candidates for that honor are Lee Kang-Baek and Oh T'ae-Sŏk.) However, Lee Yun-Taek clearly has influenced the tone and direction of Korean theater over the past two decades and, as an acknowledged theatre icon, will continue to do so. Three works in this anthology (*Citizen K*, *The Dummy Bride*, and *Mask of Fire*) provide insights into Lee's artistry and the turbulent socio-political climate in Korea during the late 1980s. The fourth play, *O-Gu*, manifests Lee's innate talents as a creator of theatre and remains an audience favorite a decade after its premiere.

In addition to obvious cultural and linguistic challenges, the translators were challenged by the Korean texts of the plays, which often exhibit Lee's focus as a creator of theatre and social criticism, rather than as a writer of dramatic literature. Stage directions often are omitted from the Korean texts, some stage directions seem to conflict with dialogue, and·Lee, as does the renowned Oh T'ae-sŏk, changes stage action and movement patterns in

ix

rehearsals so that the actual theatre event may be quite different from the written text. Thus, on occasion we have added stage directions in the translation to clarify action or to better illuminate what we believe to be Mr. Lee's intention(s). Because Mr. Lee is a poet, and his scripts have the "look" of poetry on the printed page, we also attempted to reproduce that "look" in our English version as much as possible. However, publishing cost considerations in some instances required altering the shape of, and space required by, Mr. Lee's stage directions.

Acknowledgements

The translators are grateful for a generous grant from the Korean Literature Translation Institute, without which completion of this volume would have been impossible. The Institute's project reviewer, Hugh G. Ferrar of the University of Iowa, provided valuable insights regarding the translations. Richard Nichols' travel to Seoul was supported on one occasion by grants from Penn State University's Institute for the Arts and Humanities and from the College of Arts and Architecture Associate Dean for Graduate Studies and Research. Earlier fellowships from the Korea Foundation (1998) and the Fulbright Commission (2002-3) greatly aided Richard Nichols' initial research into modern Korean theatre. Special thanks go to Judith Rothman and editor David Chao at University Press of America for publishing this work.

The translators, working half a world apart, incurred individual special debts to others. From Seoul, Dongwook Kim writes: "To my wife, Professor Seog Young-Joong who encouraged me most to undertake these translations, I'd express my deep appreciation from the bottom of my heart in 'open-silence.' What she did for me during the translation period is yet another token of her love. To Mr. Lee Yun-Taek, the author of the original plays and my close friend, I'd like to express how deeply I appreciate him, not only as an author but also as a director, a company-managing owner and producer, and a leader of the current Korean theatre. I am very proud that I live in the same age with him who is already a living legend in Korea. I would also like to thank those of his company members who gave treasured performances, especially Mrs. Lee Yun-Ju, and Ms. Kim So-Hee, among others."

Richard Nichols acknowledges ineffable gratitude to his wife, Sharleen, for her love, patience, and willingness to be a good sport, living in unfamiliar cultures away from friends and family. Many Korean theatre artists and scholars gave freely of their time and expertise in regard to this project, but these must be mentioned at the risk of slighting others: Lee Kang-Baek, Jung Jin-Soo, Kim Yun-Cheol, Sohn Jinchaek, Lee Jae-Myun, Lee Hyung-Jin, and Kim Alyssa. Thanks also are due Penn State University graduate students, Kang Younghee, Cho So-Eun and Deberniere Torrey for their insights regarding particularly difficult sections of Korean materials. Cheri Sinclair assisted with text formatting issues and Lynn Shuster provided helpful editing of the text draft.

Translators' Note

These translations are intended for a general English-speaking audience. For that reason, we chose to use the Korean Ministry of Culture and Tourisms Romanization system, rather than the McCune-Reischauer system, familiar to scholars but occasionally intimidating to the generalist because of the many diacritical marks it employs. The Ministry's system, adopted in July, 2000, has been criticized for its shortcomings, but no system meets all needs at all times and the reader will find inconsistencies in application of the Ministry system herein, most especially when published references to persons or works have used the McCune-Reischauer system (for example, Oh T'ae-Sŏk), or when a person has a personal preference (as in Sohn Jinchaek), or where a history of variant usage is present (as in Chun Doo-Whan or Rhee Syngman). The translators have sought accurate application of Ministry standards, but the system has not been long in use and we acknowledge that some inconsistencies may be our own responsibility.

Personal names in this volume are presented in Korean order, family name followed by given name(s). Koreans generally have two given names, as in Lee *Yun-Taek*, but there are exceptions. We commonly have used a hyphen between the two given names in the text, but, again, there are exceptions.

As for pronunciation, Korean syllables generally require even stress. While guidance from a native speaker is suggested, the brief pronunciation guide below may be useful. Detailed explanation of the Ministry system may be found at <http://en.wikipedia.org/wiki/Revised_romanization_of_Korean>.

Ministry System	IPA	Equivalents
i	[i] or [I]	po**li**ce
o	[ou] or [o]	g**o**
eo	[ʌ]	p**u**tt
e	[e]	n**e**t
a	[ɑ]	id**ea**l
u	[u]	t**oo**
eu	[ŭ]	p**u**t*
æ	[æ]	l**a**g
œ	No equivalent in English; Koreans may pronounce it much like the **we** in w**e**t.	

*The sound is made, not with rounded lips, but with the corners of the lips pulled back.

Some consonants are aspirated, such as "t" (**t**attle) "k" (**k**iss); the voiced sound will resemble a "d" and "g," respectively. Double consonants such as "kk" and "tt" are pronounced with greater pressure than the single consonant.

The Korean equivalent of the sound "**sh**" appears transcribed in many texts as **sh** (as in *shinpa'gŭk* and *Shilhŏm*). The Mininstry standards render the sounds as *sinpa-geuk* and *Silheom*, respectively.

Whenever possible, we have attempted to minimize use of Korean nouns or verbs within the English translation. Monetary references always present a challenge, and, in our case, we elected to use the Korean term, *won*, rather than some created equivalent. We maintained the Korean word, *kut* (using a variant Romanization because the Ministry standard, *gut*, is too easily confused with an English anatomical designation), and the shamans' chants in *O-Gu* have not been translated at all. Such chants are often unintelligible when sung in Korean; we merely Romanized the Korean sounds. Finally, there is a Korean expression, *a-i-go,* the pronunciation and meaning of which often depends on the context in which it is used. We used the Korean word, rather than attempting to convey an English-language equivalent, such as "oh, my!" or "I'm not happy."

We tried to balance an accurate representation of the source culture and language with the needs of the target audience, the reader who may have no knowledge whatsoever of Korea or Lee Yun-Taek. Whenever we had doubts (and that was often), if we erred, we erred on the side of a translation that in our estimation would provide the reader the most *theatrically* viable rendering of the text, rather than the most literary or linguistically accurate rendering.

Introduction to Contemporary Korean Theatre: Its Context

Like its neighbors, China and Japan, Korea has rich, centuries-old music and dance traditions associated with court ritual, religious observances, and village life. Traditions of mask dance dramas and puppet plays also are common, but, unlike China and Japan, Korea has no tradition of dramatic literature prior to the twentieth century.[1] Shaped by education in Confucian classics, Korean Joseon (Chosŏn) Dynasty (1392–1910) ruling and upper-classes had literary interests that included various forms of poetry, for example, but dramatic literature simply was deemed inappropriate for the educated elite. Without powerful patrons interested in literature intended for performance (such as the Japanese *noh* had in the *samurai* warrior class) and with no flourishing middle-class in a large urban area (such as supported the Beijing opera in the nineteenth and early twentieth centuries), no buildings specifically identified as theatres were built in Korea prior to the twentieth century. Korean theatre performance remained orally-transmitted and largely improvisational, whether it used masks or puppets (or both), whether the performers were village farmers or itinerant players. It was only in the last decade of the Joseon Dynasty that Western dramatic literature was introduced to Korea via Japan and China and the history of modern Korean theatre began. The following overview provides a context for the plays in this volume and Lee Yun-Taek's place in contemporary Korean theatre.

OVERVIEW

Prior to the late nineteenth century, Korea, by choice or by force, often fell under Chinese influence. That relationship permitted Korean isolationist policies,

1

earning Korea the appellation, "the Hermit Kingdom." However, in the second half of the nineteenth century, Korea, also known as "the Land of the Morning Calm," was dragged out of isolation and buffeted by political and military colonial conflicts in which it was powerless. Conservative neo-Confucian elements strove to keep Korea isolated, but were swept aside by the advance of American and European trading interests and forces of modernization, led the by the Japanese, whose aggressive plans to colonize Korea for economic and military benefit would reach fruition—with American acquiescence—in 1910 when Japan formally annexed Korea.

Modern historians debate the benefits of the Japanese occupation and the modernization that came with it, but the drive toward modernization unquestionably was a stimulus in the construction of the Hyŏmnyulsa, the first Korean indoor theatre in 1902; the first Western-style theatre, the Wŏn-gaksa, was built in 1908. Neither theatre survived long and they thus symbolize modern Korean theatre's troubled beginnings.[2]

Korean theatre's early years were shaped first by erroneous Japanese understandings of Western drama, then by Japanese colonial policies (1910–1945) intended to provide pro-Japanese propaganda and obliterate Korean culture. After the establishment of two Koreas in 1948 and through the Korean War (1950–53), rightist and leftist camps in the theatre world engaged in internecine struggles for political power that had begun even before the end of WWII. Rhee Syngman's (Yi Sŭngman, 1875–1965) accession to the presidency began a series of military-backed regimes that imposed rigid anti-communist policies, including censorship and draconian punishment of offenders, many of whom were dramatists. In the more democratic era since 1988, Lee Yun-Taek's early works appeared, causing a stir because of the socio-political criticism contained therein. Despite daunting obstacles, South Korean theatre has matured since then, as has Lee's artistry, and both justifiably are leaders in Asia's contemporary theatre community.

JAPANESE COLONIAL ERA: 1910–1945

Colonial authorities sternly repressed traditional Korean theatre forms but introduced two modern forms: the short-lived *simpageuk* (*shimp'agŭk* or "new school drama") imitating Japanese *shimpa*;[3] and *sin-geuk* (*shingŭk* or "new drama"), based on Western realism, studied and promulgated by intellectual societies such as the Dramatic Art Society (1920), and the Dramatic Art Research Society (1931), founded by Korean college students in Japan. *Sin-geuk* playwrights especially imitated works by Irish playwrights such as Synge (1871–1909) and O'Casey (1880–1964). Close imitation of non-Korean models perhaps contributed to *sin-geuk*'s later failure to capture wide audience interest in Korea (some modern commentary suggests that *sin-geuk* appealed only to an intellectual elite), but it is also true that colonial censorship limited *sin-geuk*'s development as socio-political commentary. Still, *sin-geuk*'s legacy was visible in the Korean theatre well into the 1960s.

Simpageuk was introduced around 1911. As it developed, plays based on Korean novels and popular Western novels appeared. Titles of plays such as *Dream of Lasting Resentment* (Changhanmong, 1913) and *Bitterness of a Faithful Wife* (Cheongbuweon, 1916) suggest the melodramatic themes of painful family relationships and tragic romance at the core of *simpageuk*'s popularity. Though its heyday lasted only a couple of decades, its influence continues to this day: Melodramatic, emotionally over-wrought films are characterized negatively as *"simpa,"* (*shimp'a*) but Lee Yun-Taek, as we shall see in the next chapter, today views the *simpa* legacy as a positive, integral factor in his attempts to create a "populist drama."

TRANSITIONAL PERIOD: 1945–1960

After World War II (1940–45), ideological conflict previously held in check by colonial repressive policies broke out between theatre artists. Many leftist playwrights fled to North Korea after Korea was partitioned in 1948. Though South Korea was impoverished, the National Theatre (Gungnip Geukjang), with its own company, the New Association Theatre Company (Geukdan Sinhyeop) was established in 1950, only to have the Korean conflict intervene and modern Korean theatre was taken to the brink of extinction. Only occasional performances of Shakespearean plays in and around the southeastern port city of Busan kept theatre alive during the war. Afterwards, having returned to Seoul, about fifty per cent of Sinhyeop productions were of translated Western (especially American) dramas but plays by "the father of Korean theatre," Yu Chi-Jin (1905–1974), also played a significant role. The presence, and frequent popularity, of American dramas on Seoul stages continues to this day, an aspect of Westernization in contemporary Korea that Lee Yun-Taek disparages.

KOREAN THEATRE MATURES: 1960–1988

During the 1960s, Korean observers noted many obstacles facing their theatre: insufficient numbers and types of theatres; a scarcity of theatre-savvy playwrights; meager financial resources, and so on. After all, the Korean infra-structure was in shambles and South Korea was one of the poorest nations in the world. But, modern theatre became an important vehicle for political opposition agitating for social change in the 1960s, and a Korean theatre speaking with its own "voice"—not an American or Japanese voice—emerges and matures. In the searches for a theatre both modern *and* Korean, five trends stand out: renewed respect for traditional Korean forms as resources for modern Korean theatre; great affinity for and popularity Theatre of the Absurd (Beckett's *Waiting for Godot* was and is particularly popular); inter-cultural theatre experimentation (Kim Jeong-Ok's experimentation with French classics to comment on Korean life were notable); the demise of *sin-geuk*; and the rise of the director. Small theatre groups (*tongin*) with a passion for meaningful art, not commerce, led the way.[4]

In 1960, university graduates educated in Korea, not in Japan or by the Japanese, founded the Experimental Theatre Company (Silheom Geukdan). Other theatre companies soon followed. With few places to perform, they moved into basement spaces around universities, their visible legacy today the approximately forty-five cramped underground theatres in Seoul's University Street (Taehangno) theatre district. Lee Yun-Taek's Guerilla Theatre (Gerilla Geukjang, 2004) now occupies a Taehangno site.

During the 1970s, a decade of intense creativity ensued as artists such as Choe In-Hun (1936–), Oh T'ae-sŏk, Yu Deok-Hyeong (1938–), Kim Jeong-Ok (1932–) and Lee Kang-Baek (1947–), among others, sought inventive ways to circumvent suffocating theatre censorship in order to express political dissent or social criticism. In a less structured context, *madanggeuk*, an outdoor form combining mask dance drama, folk entertainments and political content became a weapon in student-led movements against military regimes into the 1980s, uniting students and common laborers, and challenging Establishment concepts of theatre. One may find elements of *madanggeuk* in various Lee Yun-Taek writings and productions to the present day.

The 1980s brought profound change: South Korea become a formidable economic power; the repressive 1971 Performance Law was revised; world-class theatre complexes were built in Seoul; playwright/directors such as Lee Yun-Taek and Kim Kwang-Lim (1952–) came to prominence; Korean theatre artists were free to travel, undertaking international exchanges and hosting international festivals; feminist issues were addressed in the theatre; and, in 1988–89, government restrictions on theatre performance were relaxed.[5] Park Jo-Yeol's (1930–) *General Oh's Toenail* (O Changgun ui Paltop, 1974), banned for some fifteen years as a symbol of the pent-up desire for unification of the two Koreas, premiered at last and the staging of long-proscribed plays by Bertolt Brecht was permitted. Lee Yun-Taek's writings may not refer specifically to the influence of Brecht's theories and plays on his own work, but Lee's *Citizen K* suggests the influence is there, however casual it may be.

KOREAN THEATRE 1989 TO THE PRESENT: AN INTERNATIONAL PRESENCE

Seoul now is a major theatre center in Asia, hosting an international performing arts festival yearly. Koreans led the way in the establishment of the successful BeSeTo (Beijing-Seoul-Tokyo) Theatre Festival; the past president of the International Theatre Institute is Korean; Korean productions have been invited to perform in Japan, Russia, Germany, France, and the United States; Korean plays have been translated into German, Czechoslavkian, Polish, Chinese, Japanese and other languages; Korean designers have won medals at prestigious Prague exhibitions; and Korean theatre's rise to international stature is symbolized by the honors given *The Last Empress* (Myeongseong Hwanghu, 1995) during its performances in London and New York City.

Early in the 1950s, Korea had only one space suitable for theatre performance. Now there are some eighty multi-purpose performing arts centers in Korea, with another fifty or so theatres actively holding commercial performances in Seoul. Some 200 theatre companies operate in Korea today, mostly in Seoul, but some in Busan and other regional cities. Among currently (2006) active and influential companies are these: A-Com (musical theatre), Geukdan Hakcheon (Hakcheon Theatre Company, international dramas/ musicals), Gungnip Geukdan (the National Drama Company), Geukdan Michoo (Sohn Jinchaek's Michoo Theatre Company), Oh T'ae-sŏk's Mokwha Repertory Theatre Company), Geukdan Mucheon (Kim A-ra's Mucheon Theatre Company), Sanullim Theatre (since 1970), Yeonu Mudae (Yeonu Stage Company) which performs only original works) and Lee Yun-Taek's Yeonhuidan Georipae (Yeonhuidan Theatre Group), which includes his Street Theatre Troupe and other operations.[6]

Today's Korean theatre is not easily characterized and it is important to remember that it largely has been free of censorship and other repressive governmental policies for less than two decades. Like the South Korean version of democratic governance, contemporary Korean theatre still is in the process of maturing. Of course, there are growing pains: Productions of translated Western works still represent a significant portion of performances each year (about one-third, down from the long-time level of about one-half). Critics suggest that postmodern theories have prevented some young Korean playwrights from learning how to tell a story *dramatically*. A productive tension between high quality dramatic criticism, playwriting, and theatre performance is not yet common in

Seoul. Some directors increasingly disregard the playwright's text in favor of their own concepts and, in response, playwrights direct their own plays with increasing frequency, further limiting artistic cross-fertilization. Mature actors largely have deserted the live theatre in favor of television and film. The small theatres in Seoul do not permit long runs in the same theatre (runs average about two weeks), so the artists involved do not have time to develop and there seldom is time enough for box office income to off-set production expenditures. Government subsidies for theatre productions have eased financial worries only slightly. As in any theatre center, including New York and London, the future of Korean theatre (other than musicals, which dominate the commercial theatre in Seoul) is a topic of debate among critics and artists.

To exert greater control over the creative process and artistic product, artists such as Sohn Jinchaek, Oh T'ae-Sŏk, Kim Kwang-Lim and Lee Yun-Taek have formed their own production units, complete with actor training programs. University theatre departments also are forming alliances with certain director/producers and companies. Some observers applaud the trends just noted and find hope in the greater sophistication and diversity in Seoul audiences. One certainly senses a positive energy in the theatre district's atmosphere, and, despite all the obstacles, in any given week can find performances that would grace stages in New York or London.

Lee Yun-Taek was at the forefront of experimental, socially conscious theatre in the late 1980s, but, since the early 1990s, experimental productions have waned and contemporary Korean theatre generally is less politically conscious than it was in the previous two decades. Lee's *O-Gu* has been a popular tourist attraction at Seoul's Cheongdong Theatre and made into a film (*O-Gu: Hilarious Mourning,* 2003) with none of the darker elements of *O-Gu*'s earlier stage versions or the biting intellect found in *The Dummy Bride*, *Citizen K*, and *Mask of* Fire. Lee's works these days, whether as a writer or a director/producer, seem decidedly more main-stream than they once were, though one may debate whether his work is less controversial, especially his productions that deconstruct history or Western theatre classics. His complex artistic imprint, in all its many forms, is a highly visible, clear path in the landscape of contemporary Korean theatre and, with his 2004 appointment as artistic director of the National Theatre of Korea's Drama Company, will continue to be so for the foreseeable future. His career to date is the subject of the next chapter.

NOTES:

1. The texts for *pansori*, a sung narrative performed by a solo singer supported by a drummer, are adaptations of classic novels, the remaining five versions of which

were given literary form by an educated aficionado, Shin Chae-Hyo (1812–84), to increase *pansori*'s esteem in the eyes of the literati.

2. The Cheongdong Theatre in central Seoul, built in 1995, advertises itself as a theatre continuing the founding philosophy of the Wŏn-gaksa, but these days, little modern drama is performed at the Cheongdong. The theatre specializes in traditional music, theatre, and dance presentations for foreign tourists and Korean school children.

3. *Shimpa* was a melodramatic amalgam of traditional Japanese *kabuki* domestic drama and modern drama, Japanese style.

4. Insights from Kim Ah-jeong, Kim Yun-Cheol and Lee Hye-Kyung are combined in this paragraph and acknowledged.

5. Strict film censorship continued until 1999.

6. Governmentally promulgated transliteration standards are not widely used in the Korean theatre world. For example, variants of Hakcheon, Hakchon, and Hakjeon are used and Geuktan ("theatre company") is more often transliterated as Kuktan or Kukdan.

Lee Yun-Taek: A Brief Biography

Lee Yun-Taek's Street Theatre Troupe Web site describes him as "a 'culture guerilla,' an artist frequently at the forefront of diverse genres, his titles including poet, playwright, television writer, screen play writer, theatre director and, most recently, film director."[i] Iconoclastic and charismatic, Lee Yun-Taek is an artist whose each creative endeavor is awaited eagerly then debated heatedly by critics. Well-known for evocative stage imagery, audacious artistic inspiration, and bold use of color and composition, Lee also captures essences of humanity in poignant vignettes such as the granddaughter's chat with the Messenger from Hell in *O-Gu* and the Dummy Bride's elegiac longing for her home village "this side of the sky." On the other hand, his original plays and adaptations of Western classics have struck some Korean critics as didactic and excessively wordy, with seemingly unconnected or unnecessary episodes. Watching his productions of *Oedipus* (2002), *The Tempest* (2002), and *The Merchant of Venice* (2003), I wondered if he had closely read the original versions—but then, Lee, never claimed fidelity to the originals. Defying easy classification, his works run the gamut from *O-Gu*'s joyful, warm optimism to *Citizen K*'s dark pessimism to *The Tempest*'s saccharine romanticism. However one feels about Lee Yun-Taek's writing and stage directing, he unquestionably is a singularly influential figure in the Korean theatre world today.

The four plays in this anthology represent only his developing artistry within the socio-political realities in South Korea, 1989–1993, and should not be viewed as accurate representations of the entirety of Lee Yun-Taek's extraordinary artistic output. However, his affection for Korea, her people and her culture, his earthy, passionate life-force, empathy for the lonely, distrust of authoritarianism, and his ability to find truthful humor in emotionally-charged moments are qualities visible in these four plays and they inform subsequent works to this day.

Now at the apex of the Korean theatre world as artistic director of the Drama Company at the National Theatre of Korea, Lee's career spans twenty years since he founded the Street Theatre Troupe (Yeonhuidan Keoripae) in his home city of Busan in 1986, staging minimalist productions in the cramped Gamagol Theatre. His 1989 production of *Citizen K* (Shinmin K) in Seoul's Dongsoong Art Center immediately and powerfully impressed itself on audiences and critics alike, an augury of the intensity and often controversial nature of his subsequent theatre endeavors. In the intervening years, he has staged some seventy theatre productions of his own works and others, including Lee Kang-Baek's *A Feeling, Like Nirvana* (Neukkim, Geungnyak Gateun, 1998), Kim Kwang-Lim's *Hong Dong-Ji is Alive* (Hong Dong-Ji neun Sala itta, 1993), and Oh T'ae-Sŏk's *A Vinyl House* (Binil Hasueu, 1994). Additionally, he published anthologies of his poetry and plays, a long novel, a critical biography of Kafka and collections of criticism, authored influential texts on his method of actor training and playwriting, established the U-ri Theatre Institute, the Milryang Theatre Village outside of Busan and the Guerilla Theatre in Seoul's Taehangno theatre district, and taught in some of Korea's leading theatre departments. In two decades, his restless, creative energies have earned him some twenty theatre awards and led him to a true "star" status in Korea and considerable international recognition in Asia and Europe, especially in Germany where his productions have received critical acclaim. However, he remains largely unknown in the United States and there is only scant information in English about his life and works.

Born in Busan in 1952, Lee entered the Seoul Theatre Institute in 1972, but dropped out in that same year. Graduating from the Korean National Open University in 1979 with a degree in elementary education, he joined the newspaper, *Busan Ilbo* (Busan News), as a reporter, working in that capacity until 1986, an experience reflected in the auto-biographical tone and content of his *Citizen K*.

Lee describes himself as a cultural anarchist, unwilling to be oppressed by "rules" of art, and, most especially, unwilling to submit to American cultural hegemony and the theatre realism that has dominated Korean stages until only recently. Some theatre critics and artists other than Lee have come to believe that realism is inimical to a Korean aesthetic and has stunted the growth of a truly *Korean* theatre. To neutralize (if not negate) Western realism's stultifying effects, Lee and other leading creators of theatre, such as Sohn Jinchaek and Oh T'ae-sŏk, look for Korean cultural "DNA" in traditional forms, such as folk mask-dance plays (*talchum*), puppetry (*kkoktu-kakshi* and *baltal*), farmer's music (*no-ak*), *madangnori* and shamanistic ritual (*kut*). Lee employs aspects of these forms to replace theatrical realism's statement-like serial lines, scenic verisimilitude, specific times and spaces, linear storyline, and in-depth portrayal of a central character, instead utilizing vocal patterns and intonations, music, dance, imagery (both poetic and visual) and audience involvement through direct address and other devices to deconstruct surface reality in order to reach the reality under the surface.[2]

Oh T'ae-sŏk (Lee's senior by about ten years) is known for using Korean *traditional* stories in unorthodox ways to comment upon contemporary Korean life. Lee Yun-Taek and his Street Theatre Troupe often seek out *Western* classics to perform in a Korean style. His works based on Shakespearean and Greek classics are known, even notorious, for their deconstruction of history *and* the given classic play on which his production is based. His *Hamlet* (1998) was lauded in Germany for its fresh interpretation of the play, but other works have been criticized for seemingly paying little heed to the original text, as in his adaptation of *Oedipus* in which the classic story was lost in a collage of projected photographs from twentieth century Korean history or a production of *The Merchant of Venice* at Sungkyunkwan University done in contemporary dress and featuring and hip-hop influenced music and dance.

Lees' search for a thoroughly Korean form of theatre does not exclude experimentation with appropriate elements of Western theatre and literature. Plays by Bertolt Brecht were forbidden in South Korea until after 1988, but his theories—and those of Artaud, along with the works of European Absurdists—were well-known in theatre circles. There is a Brechtian quality in Lee's use of projections to announce scenes and provide pertinent details in *Citizen K*, an "agit-prop" aspect in the intellectual debates about power in *Mask of Fire*, Absurdist elements in his use of humans as puppets and puppets as humans in *The Dummy Bride*, and, his adaptations of Kafka's works remain repertoire mainstays, most recently an adaptation of *The Metamorphosis* performed again at the Guerilla Theatre in Seoul in December 2004.

Such experimentation may seem quite intellectual and contrary to Lee's view of himself as a petit bourgeoisie—that is, an anti-intellectual—thus one must consider a tendency in Lee's work seen by the critic, Lee Hye-Kyung: the tendency to popularize Korean theatre, to remove it from control of an intellectual elite and return it to the audience.[3] That desire may not be obvious in *Citizen K* and *Mask of Fire* (though some critics suggest that the raw sex and nudity in both productions contributed to increased attendance), but glimpses may be seen in *The Dummy Bride*, and clearly are manifest in *O-Gu*, in which farce, comedy, sentimental situations, age-old ritual, folk and modern music, and active audience involvement are mixed to create a "populist play." Lee, according to Lee Hye-Kyung, wants to make the theatre "more familiar to the public by awakening that penchant for play, ritual and feast latent in the collective consciousness of the people."[4] And it is a sign of Lee's complex artistic vision that this man with so many post-modern tendencies finds artistic stimulation in a sentimental, emotionally overwrought theatre form, *sinpa-geuk,* popular in Korea decades ago (ca. 1912–1930s). Lee has written that *sinpa,* because of its Japanese origins, should no longer be applied to the melodramatic mixture of comedy, pathos, song and dance that his more recent works especially represent. Rather, he prefers a term without Western or Japanese connotations: *tejung yeon-geuk,* a non-realistic, epic "populist theatre," which invites the audience to empathize with the actors and to feel free emotionally.[5] Even his musical version of *The Tempest,* with a lush emotional score by Zdeněk Barták and Kim Dae-Seong and pre-opening sales of sound track DVDs, was designed to touch the sentiments of the young audience. Darker (more literary?) themes in Shakespeare's work, such as the passing of generations and the battle between nature and civilization were minimized.

For some, there may be seeming disconnect between Lee's intention to popularize the theatre and an essential quality in some of his plays, especially the three "ceremony" plays in this anthology.[6] Lee wishes for theatre to become once again important to the populace and a place for open debates about Korean society, but communication between author and receiver in his plays may strike one as one-directional: From *auteur*/director to reader/audience member. The long speeches in *Citizen K* and *Mask of Fire* may seem more like lectures than dialogue to a Western reader. Now, some of Lee's contemporaries, playwrights Lee Kang-Baek, Kim Kwang-Lim, and Lee Man-Hui (1954–) among them, also use long speeches; Korean audiences seem much more tolerant of the wordiness than Westerners might be (though certain of Moliere's works are infamous for the length of characters' speeches). However, in Lee Yun-Taek's case, long speeches in *Mask of Fire,* for example, often are used to *explain* rhetorically, rather than to portray or advance characterization, a tendency that, from this observer's perspective, seems to exclude audience participation, rather than inviting it.

Korean responses to Lee's works aside, a Westerner encountering the works in this anthology may well question their relevance to a Westerner. After all, they are generally *Asian,* specifically *Korean.* However, the reader who spends a little time and effort to move by the temporary, surface obstacles presented by Korean names, locales, history, social setting and other elements may be rewarded by glimpses into Lee Yun-Taek's humanistic imagination and the portrayal of universal truths not limited by geographic boundaries. The plays in this collection are not subtle; individual characters are not deeply developed; plots are not complex. But, there is an implacable moral vision informing each play and, to this writer, Lee's vision of the world deserves attention because, in a world where "politically correct spin" is everywhere, Lee comes at the world straight on.

NOTES:

1. Street Theatre Troupe, <web site. http://www.stt1986.com/STT_NEW> (20 Apr. 2006).

2. Lee Hye-Kyung. "Yi, Yun-Taek." in *Contemporary Korean Theatre*, ed. Korean Association of Theatre Critics. (Seoul: Theatre and Man Press, 2000), 155–166.

3. ———.

4. ———.

5. Lee Yun-Taek. *Theatre Works* (Yeongeuk Jakeop). Theatre program in my possession, dated February 9, 2003.

6. The Korean word, *hyeong-shik*, is part of the subtitles for all the plays in this anthology except for *Citizen K*. The word means "form" or "style," but the translators prefer to use a related meaning, "ceremony," to reinforce a sense of theatre ritual clearly present in the texts.

Introduction to *Citizen K*

Citizen K (Sinmin K, 1989) reflects Lee Yun-Taek's seven years as a reporter for the *Busan News* during the repressive, unpopular regime of President Chun Doo-Whan (Chŏn Tu-Whan, 1932–) from 1981–1988. The play's title and the implied contrast to Orson Welle's classic, *Citizen Kane*, needs no explication. Indeed, the play itself is without guile or subtlety, a series of vignettes arranged in an epic, Living Newspaper fashion, not to illuminate character but to expose a situation, to shock and provoke a visceral audience response. There are no scenes in the play; there are episodes, their titles indicating the simple, almost crude, structure of the play: Prologue, Announcement, An Inquiry, Torture, Ideological Struggle—In the Prison Cell, Ideological Struggle—At the Trial, Everyday Life Itself was Arrested, Epilogue. The Interrogator in the play says, "each of the dramatic personae in this play is an individual person as well as a figure representing a given social class in our time," but Lee has written character *types* (including Citizen K) that are one-dimensional, stereotypic images with no relevant past and no informing future. They are mere cogs in the abusive, militaristic and inhumane political machinery that destroys the ambivalent—and hardly courageous—poet and intellectual, Citizen K. Lee's audience did not need great character detail to experience empathy; the work on stage resembled all too clearly what they knew personally or had heard about.

It must be remembered that the period 1980–88 began with Chun Doo-Whan's illegal assumption of control of the Korean Central Intelligence Agency and the subsequent full scale insurrection by students and common citizens in the city of Gwanju (Kwangju), ultimately put down by crack paratroopers, at the cost of at least 200 lives (some estimates go as high as 2,000 deaths). The advancing decade was marked by martial law, dissolution of the

National Assembly, the banning of labor strikes and the shuttering of all colleges and universities. Criticism of the government was a punishable offense; newspapers were frequently censored or shut down. Leaders of opposition parties were jailed on spurious charges, including sedition, punishable by death. Student demonstrations were common and there were massive, violent confrontations with riot police. Torture, though its existence was denied by the Chun government, was a common tactic used by police and secret police alike. A Seoul National University student leader, Park Jong-Cheol (Park Chong-Ch'ŏl) died during an interrogation in 1987 and a wave of street fighting between demonstrators and police broke over the nation's cities. An eight-point reform platform forwarded by Roh Tae-Woo in June, 1988, promulgating direct presidential elections, restoration of civil rights, lifting of press restrictions and other reforms was accepted by Chun. The wave of violence subsided and an era of more open government began. It was in the early days of that more open government that Lee Yun-Taek was able to write *Citizen K.*

Political realities outside of Korea also are evidenced in Lee's play. The sudden overthrow of the Marcos government in the Philippines, February 1986, fueled to some extent Korean hopes that direct popular agitation could lead to positive political change. Chun earlier had threatened to jail anyone signing petitions in favor of constitutional revisions, but, in the face of the Philippine situation, altered his stance, agreeing to constitutional change at the end of his presidency in 1988. However, he soon reversed himself again, only adding fuel to the combustible conditions noted just above. In the section of *Citizen K* titled "Statement of the Right-Wing Intellectual," Lee reminds the audience that, though the political situation indeed had improved, fundamental human rights guarantees were still not provided by the government.

Citizen K is the first of his "ceremony" plays and exhibits characteristics found in subsequent works. First, his "characters" are nameless; they are defined by title or function—not by personal names. Second, the ideas expounded by the "characters" are not so much *their* ideas as they are one aspect of an intellectual analysis or political statement Lee is making through and with them. Third, Lee has a propensity to use lengthy monologues, rather than characters in action, speaking dialogue, to crystallize and drive home central ideas and themes. Unlike realistic drama where character action leads to a gradual formation of themes or motifs, Lee relies on long speeches, often in solitude, to *tell* the audience what he wants featured and understood. See, for example, the Actor A/Interrogator's two-page speech in Episode 3 of *Citizen K.* Fourth, comedy is an irrepressible and welcome aspect of Lee's writing (take, for example, the Female Reporter's line—as she and Citizen K wait in terror for the police—that she'd like to go shopping!). Fifth, Lee often reminds audience members that they are not to be passive observers, sitting outside some aesthetic "fourth wall." He uses direct, often ironic, address to the audience to keep the viewer engaged in the examination of ideas taking place on stage:

> Interrogator: The investigator role I took represents ultra-right wing intellectuals.
> Citizen K: How about we drop it for now and get back to the play?
> Interrogator: Please bear in mind that the exercise of overwhelming force is also an appropriately targeted strategy for treating those from the learned classes, which means tell me the truth without killing any more time!
> Citizen K: Oh, shut up! The play must go on, as the script says.

Sixth, in the "ceremony" plays, Lee features violence, much of it sexual. One may well argue that the plays deal with violent abuse of power and thus the stage violence is justified. Still, the sexual grappling that concludes Episode 1 in *Citizen K*, for example, seems more prurient than dramatic. Lastly, Lee writes powerful *scenarios* for socio-political purposes; he does not write dramatic *literature*. He envisions events on stage that are only suggested by the words of the play, not, as in realistic dramatic literature, contained within the words. That said, the closing stage direction in *Citizen K* is hauntingly poetic, presaging Lee's published collections of poetry and his current renown as a creator of striking visual stage imagery.

Citizen K

Dramatis Personae: *(*In general order of appearance.*)*

    Citizen K, a reporter

    Chief Editor

    Female Reporter

    Reporter Choe

    Interrogator

    Ex-Investigator General

    Judge

    Female College Student

    Female Singer-Prostitute

    Citizen K's reporter colleagues

    Torturer

    Jailor

Performers:

Citizen K

Actor A *re-creates the repressive situation during the 1980s, playing multiple roles, such as a chief editor, military inspector-interrogator, an ex-Inspector General (who is an assassin), and a judge.*

Actor B *takes two roles: a female reporter and a female college student.*

Actor C *takes roles such as: reporter Choe (the Intellectual), a torturer and a jailor.*

Actor D *takes roles as an announcer and a female singer-prostitute.*

Off-Stage Crew:

Stage Manager *(serves as light board operator as well)*

Sound Board Operator *(controls the slide projector as well)*

House Manager *(takes care of tickets and checks on the performance in process)*

* This script for a small theatre is composed of eight episodes performed by five actors and three crew members changing roles as necessary.

Performance Notes:

1. In the reading of the script, if one does not take into account Korean sound patterns in such things as recitation, monotonous reports, broadcasting style, singing and shouting, the play will be diminished as a work of fiction. The director must transform the script with quickly paced dialogue and variety in staging.

2. If there is no calculation for dynamic character transformation in the actors and a plan for shifting stage props in the scene changes, blackouts which interrupt progress and unnecessary noises will reduce the theatrical tension.

3. The actors need total identification with the characters, rather than being attached to their own individual personalities.

4. Sound, lighting design and slide projections are not mere dramatic accessories, but essential devices which, because they play a role in weaving the dramatic context for the play, must not be overlooked.

PROLOGUE

A heavy snow falls to earth.

In the prologue, some evidence of reconstructed realistic materials is a reminder of the repression of the 1980s. These testaments are delivered through slide-film projections, songs, broadcast announcements, and some actors' dialogue. These audio-visual "languages" delivered in various ways are emblems which symbolize the restrictive situation of South Korean politics and her history in the1980s. These materials, therefore, are real, no, not just real, but a theatrical language beyond reality.

Prologue in largo,
"House" lights out.
Actors enter with the music and. . .

Projections 1–3: *(Excerpts from newspaper headlines, May 1980).*

1. Gwangju under martial law/Assassin Kim Jae-Kyu gets death sentence.[1]
2. In emergency measure, the National Security Committee is launched/ Operates to maintain national order.
3. National Intelligence Service purges more than 300 people/Martial commander issues all-points bulletin for 329 suspects.

(Projections end. Blackness.)

Singing. (The performers sing in the darkness.)
   Kiss of fire to melt the snow,
   Kiss and say farewell to comfort my heart,
   Snow falls on that lonely pine,
   Your forehead lonely lies beneath my hair.
   Simone, your brother's eyes fall closed in the garden.
   Simone, you are my eyes and my love.[2]

Projections 4–5:

4. Seven newspapers cease publishing indefinitely.
5. Winter rain falls. Everywhere. . . . Storm warning for the east-west areas in the South Sea.[3]

(Blackout.)

Broadcast announcement:

"Now, clearing away the old era, we welcome a new era pledged to the construction of a just, democratic nation. To support that pledge, with a view to social welfare, we are ready to assist in the re-structuring of the mass media and broadcasting systems, as they have requested." *(Culture and Public Information Bureau news release.)*

ACTOR D: *(To the audience.)* "This paper is the last issue of the Jayu Ilbo. Subscribers, farewell. Established thirty three years, two months, and twenty-five days ago, we terminate publication with issue number 10992. Proud to have been a recorder of history and of service to our valued subscribers, our staff bids goodbye to all our readers. Even though the Jayu Ilbo is on the way to extinction, the memory of our readers will never die. Please remember us as kindly as you have supported us in the past." *(Quoted on the first page of the Kukje Newspaper's closing statement.)* [4]

Lights come up on stage.
ACTORS A, B, C *silently read newspapers.*
CITIZEN K *begins reading a newspaper aloud.*

CITIZEN K: *(Muttering to himself.)* The weather forecast changes from fog alert to storm warnings in the South Sea area at 06:00. Heavy snow with strong northwest winds, and rain; the scarlet-tinged leaves from the maple trees fall sluggishly. At 10:00, the amount of rainfall was 36 mm. Ferries to the shuttle islands of the South Sea have been cancelled. All port activity is suspended. −5°C. in the morning, 10°C. during the day.[5] With some chilly weather, we are entering the long, dark tunnel of winter. It's time for home owners to prepare winterization plans. Since the price of petroleum and electricity will rise as of the nineteenth of the month, the public's outlook is quite gloomy. *(CITIZEN K folds the newspaper, then, to the audience.)* The last article I wrote was a weather forecast. That day, it was snowing. Yes, it was an unusual first snow in the south port area. The snow in the south area is not a large flake, but is a kind of sleet, usually with rain, which soaks our shoulders and takes our breath away. With this snow, then, we had to enter the long, dark tunnel of winter. It was not such snow that I missed. Snow should be an intense white which surpasses all colors, and I dreamed of the earth on which the warm and pure blessings from the heaven poured. *(Pause.)* I went out in the street in order to take snapshots of snow, and wrote a weather report that day, adding some romantic comments about the pictures. *(Reciting.)* The snow, as if it would bear silent witness to the cries of separation, is falling on me now. Falling, falling down on the brownish sea and on the ashen-colored city. Fluttering down to the ground, on which the sun will be bright.

(Enter ACTOR A/CHIEF EDITOR.)

ACTOR A/EDITOR: *(To* CITIZEN K.*)* Images of the leaves falling slug-gishly or not is not a reporter's view, but your own. *(Pulling down his glasses.)* "We . . . are entering . . . the long, dark . . .tunnel of winter . . . "What kind of joke is this? If you really want to write a lyrical report, you should write it this way: "We are entering into the winter of the Year of the Tiger." Why do you fob off your personal views on the reader? Isn't the reporter's fundamental duty to recount the current social situation objectively to readers, rather than cooking up a touching conclusion? Why do you make me needlessly repeat lectures about newspaper style right up to the very moment the paper is being shut down?

CITIZEN K: I thought that reporting style should vary according to the social situation.

EDITOR: Oh, I get it. I'm supposed to be moved in the moment by your distinguished style. You know, if you really want to communicate meaning between the lines, you should use more concrete and realistic metaphors. Come on! Do you think readers will buy your naïve sentimentality? In my opinion, there is a fatal flaw in the headline, too. "The snow" . . . let's see . . . "would bear silent witness to the cries of separation. . ." What the hell is this? "Fluttering down to the ground"?! and "on which the sun will be bright"? . . . Isn't that a quote from the song by Kim Min-Kee?[6]

CITIZEN K: It's from the poem by Oh Jang-Hwan.[7]

EDITOR: Oh Jang-Hwan, the poet during the Japanese colonization?

CITIZEN K: Yes, that's him.

EDITOR: Are we colonized now? Referring to Oh is a kind of defeatism.

Silence.

CITIZEN K: What's going to happen to us?

EDITOR: . . .

CITIZEN K: What's going to happen to me?

EDITOR: That's not my business. *(Pause.)* Nobody can foresee the future of our newspaper, now. *(Pause.)* A barbaric age is coming. *(Pause.)* But, uh, reporters are here to stay, no matter what kind of age is coming. Keep that in mind. Nobody can eliminate us, nobody. *(ACTOR A exits.)*

Blue cyc for the scene change.

Actors move on-stage for the change, banging folding chairs as a sound effect.

EPISODE 1. ANNOUNCEMENT

The clear sound of typewriting;
an electric light with a lampshade is the only light.
On the table, there are some books, a glass, a newspaper, etc.—
Indications of a learned person—and CITIZEN K.
We can guess now that this is his room.
Knocking,
Urgent knocking.

CITIZEN K: Who is it?

ACTOR B/FEMALE REPORTER: It's me! *(Enter* ACTOR B.*)*

CITIZEN K: It's time for work already? *(Looking at his clock.)* It's so early!

FEMALE REPORTER: Don't go to work!

CITIZEN K: A reporter with no paper to publish, sitting at his desk killing time. . . it's awkward.

FEMALE REPORTER: The reporter, Mr. Choe, was arrested last night.

CITIZEN K: . . .

FEMALE REPORTER: I'm sure that it's a screening process to ferret out manifesto signatories.

CITIZEN K: You know I'm not one of them. I am not that brave.

FEMALE REPORTER: You are implicated, though.

CITIZEN K: I only typed a rough draft of the manifesto you all wrote! What was my role that day? Did I revise any sentences, erase unnecessary adjectives to mold them into a propagandistic style like a professional grammarian? Mr. Choe called me an opportunist, you know. *(What follows is a flashback, a scene that took place on the night* CITIZEN K *was visited by a reporter and revolutionary intellectual,* CHOE, *played by* ACTOR C, *who now enters.)*

ACTOR C/CHOE: *(To* CITIZEN K.*)* There is no consciousness of history in your writing. It is illusory to deal with the historical role of intellectuals with articles about the grievances of the troubled, petty bourgeois. Get it in your head with the downfall of the 4.19 generation means.[8] Limited knowledge about opportunists cannot be ameliorated until the burden of the moronic modernist's debris is cleared away. Take this chance to restore political consciousness.

CITIZEN K: *(A refutation.)* Did I inhale carbon monoxide? Am I unconscious? Then, who are you? Are you anti-government? If you're a revolutionary intellectual, why do you work for a government newspaper company instead of joining the student demonstrators scrumming in the street? You bastard! From whom do you earn the money that pays for your booze? We are already slaves to this governmental system, understand? We all are under suspicion. Your intellect is used like coins tossed by the rich to the poor. It's a sop to reduce discontent isn't it?[9] What's the difference between you and me, that we are discussing ideology dividing two groups? Huh? You're a hypocrite!

FEMALE REPORTER: *(A vindication.)* In these barbaric days, even hypocritical knowledge is better than nothing. *(Exit* ACTOR C/CHOE.*)*

CITIZEN K *and* ACTOR B/FEMALE REPORTER *exit in blackout. Lights up on stage.*
Enter CITIZEN K *and* ACTOR B/FEMALE REPORTER.

CITIZEN K: I don't understand yet why Mr. Choe tried to win me over at the very moment the first draft of the manifesto was being completed. Did he need me because I am a poet, or because he needed a kind of editor to revise the style. Ah, I see it all now! I have a typewriter! On the night the manifesto was being completed, why did all of you barge into my place? Because of this typewriter. I'm sure that you barged in to use my typewriter, and I unwittingly joined the ranks struggling to win democratic freedom of speech.

ACTOR B/FEMALE REPORTER: Please don't put yourself down that way!

CITIZEN K: Then, what is this all about? Why did Choe, a reporter who usually despises me, try to hook me into completing the manifesto? In your way of thinking was I a battlefront ally? Hadn't you nearly finished the manifesto with him? I was just for show.

FEMALE REPORTER: You are *the* fighter for democracy!

CITIZEN K: No, I'm not. I couldn't be with you at the head of the struggle. I was scared. I couldn't give up two things: compensation for a lifetime of hardships; and my wishy-washy behavior. I really wanted to build a home as others did. *(Pause.)* I wanted you to be my wife, not as a female reporter, but a housewife adorning the breakfast table. But, these days, you've plunged into issues of justice and morality. You probably are not interested at all in a coward like me.

FEMALE REPORTER: What will you do?

CITIZEN K: Well, I probably will be taken somewhere, and beaten up. Damn it! I'm not sure how I'll act in that situation. *(Desperately.)* I'm frightened of the cowardice in me.

FEMALE REPORTER: Cheer up. Things will work out fine.

CITIZEN K: You and Choe don't get it! We are not college students hauled in by the police during some demonstration. Being a college student is a kind of free pass in this society, you know, and not available to us, the general public.

FEMALE REPORTER: The five members gathered that day will be wanted soon. I'm sure that some insider is pointing the finger at us. Let's get out of this city and hide for a while.

CITIZEN K: With you? *(Sarcastically.)* What a wonderful honeymoon it would be! In this small country, where should we go to hide?

FEMALE REPORTER: We should do something to evade arrest, shouldn't we?

CITIZEN K: Choe is apprehended already, and you ask me to run away. You are treating me like an opportunist!

FEMALE REPORTER: Running away is not an act of cowardice; it is meaningless for us to stay if we will be victims of a wrongful system.

CITIZEN K: Let's wait. Take a seat and wait just like this. *(Turns off the lamp on the table.)*

A pantomime indicates the elapse of time.

CITIZEN K: Come, come quickly, and punish me.

FEMALE REPORTER: Why is the world getting so dark?

CITIZEN K: Damn it! Come what may, please release me from this suffocating fear!

FEMALE REPORTER: It's too dark, please draw back the curtain.

CITIZEN K: Not a chance. I don't want you to see how frightened I am.

FEMALE REPORTER: When will they come?

CITIZEN K: Are those sons of bitches lost and unable to find my apartment address?

FEMALE REPORTER: I don't know if Choe can hold out and insist to the end that he was the sole leader.

CITIZEN K: That's impossible!

FEMALE REPORTER: *(Pause.)* What do you say we go shopping downtown?

CITIZEN K: What the hell are you talking about at a moment like this?

FEMALE REPORTER: I'd rather be slaughtered in a brightly lit street.

CITIZEN K: Did you hear the squeaking sound at the gate of the apartments?

FEMALE REPORTER: I didn't ever have a chance to go out with you.

CITIZEN K: You've been so busy.

FEMALE REPORTER: I want to go shopping.

CITIZEN K: You usually ran around with the reporter Choe.

FEMALE REPORTER: He was a radical upperclassman in college.

CITIZEN K: You two could be a nice pair.

FEMALE REPORTER: I wanted to follow in his footsteps.

CITIZEN K: Listen, they're coming. I heard their footsteps on the stairs!

FEMALE REPORTER: I love you.

CITIZEN K: You condemned me for being an opportunist.

FEMALE REPORTER: Not me. But, the world saw you as one.

CITIZEN K: Damn it, those sons of bitches! What are they waiting for? Come on, break down the door!

FEMALE REPORTER: We've known each other for years.

CITIZEN K: So you've come! *(To those whose footsteps he hears.)*

FEMALE REPORTER: Haven't we?

K embraces her hysterically.
Their sexual grappling looks like tough human beings fighting.
A sudden reaction, an impulse of terror and repression, then three flash-light beams cut through the dark like razors.
Big men with cropped hair stand there like statues.
A naked couple is thrown down at center stage.
Black out.

EPISODE 2. AN INQUIRY

Lights up.
An INTERROGATOR (ACTOR A) in a military uniform.
It's very strange that there is no badge of rank, or name tag on it.
The look is distinctively Korean, however.

ACTOR A/INTERROGATOR: Did you sign the freedom of speech manifesto distributed in April last year?

CITIZEN K: I guess so.

INTERROGATOR: What do you mean, "I *guess* so"?

CITIZEN K: Yes, I signed it. However it was the decision of all staff members rather than my own personal decision.

INTERROGATOR: Then, you mean that you never signed on it directly?

CITIZEN K: To put it more precisely, I never wrote my name on it.

INTERROGATOR: *(Giving him a sheet of blank paper.)* Then you may go home after writing here a simple statement of, "Signing the mani-festo was not my personal decision" and "I never signed it."

CITIZEN K: *(Pause.)* Would you think about it and put yourself in my shoes, please?

INTERROGATOR: Meaning what?

CITIZEN K: Suppose you are in my situation. If I go back home after giving you that simple statement, I will be treated as traitor, and my social life will be buried. *(Pause.)* It would be better for me to go jail.

INTERROGATOR: Do you think so?

CITIZEN K: *(Irresistibly making excuses.)* I understand your job. My job, reporting, which I do for a living, is a tough job, too. It was at a newspaper company that I got a job after graduation from college. *(K's excuses come quickly.)* Do you think I have done my job with a reporter's special morality or anything like that? I guess it would be same for you. We all do what we can for a living and, how can I say this, we have some moral choices to make about what kind of job one has. So I don't want to have any hard feelings toward you. Because you're simply doing your job. Therefore, please understand what I did in regard to signing the manifesto. We have different jobs, but we're met here face to face. Once we get out of here, we may drink *soju*[10] together at some street stall. So what do you say? Let's clear up this unpleasant situation as quickly as possible. I will help you. If my signature violated the National Security law, I plead guilty. Please send me to jail, now. However, I'd like to get out of here without any hard feelings toward you. Please type my statement as you wish, and I will sign it. *(The* INTERROGATOR *guffaws, and punches* CITIZEN K *in the mouth.)*

CITIZEN K: Don't do that, please!

INTERROGATOR: "Don't do that," you said. Do you think I'm kidding now? Knock off the fucking melodramatic act and answer me, truthfully. *(He thrusts out a sheave of papers. In it is the first draft of the manifesto typewritten by* CITIZEN K.)

INTERROGATOR: "Our position on attaining democratic speech." Is this the first draft you made?

CITIZEN K: . . .

ACTOR A/INTERROGATOR *abruptly kicks K in the jaw. Falling down,* CITIZEN K *screams.*

CITIZEN K: I am a poet, a real poet, you know!

INTERROGATOR: So. . . ?

CITIZEN K: No, I was a grammarian; no, wait, I was typist. A typist!

ACTOR A/INTERROGATOR kicks K's back lightly.

INTERROGATOR: Did you pee your pants? Get up, now. We need to explain something about the next scene for the audience. *(ACTOR A explains about right wing intellectuals in our age.)*

INTERROGATOR: My role, as you see, is that of an interrogator, which, in other words, means a bad guy in general. But if my role represents merely a villain, this play would be a dull one about torture. What the author intends is that this play be seen as a social drama, which means that each of the dramatic personae in this play is an individual person as well as a figure representing a given social class in our time. *(Pointing at CITIZEN K.)* That actor now represents the young intellectuals in our society, who might be called the intellectual *nouveau riche*, so to speak. And I am not supposed to represent an illiterate military investigator, even though I might look like it with this military uniform and crewcut. I am a solid intellectual, too, with some knowledge and patriotism. It would be very helpful to think of me as ex-ROTC or a military academy graduate. My hobbies during my school days were soccer or reading books. That's why, in my own way, *(Refers to CITIZEN K.)* I can figure out what that coward poet-reporter is talking about.

CITIZEN K: Do you know who Seo Jung-Ju is? [11] You probably don't know such works as "A Poem for a Flower" by Kim Chun-Su? [12]

INTERROGATOR: My part is smart enough to read and analyze Kim Su-Yeong's poems, and Kim Ji-Ha's *Five Enemies*. [13] *(To audience, referring to CITIZEN K.)* Besides, I am a reader of that half-baked poet, too.

CITIZEN K: I am flattered . . .

INTERROGATOR: Of course, I became a reader of that poet's works only in recent months. For professional reasons! Unfortunately, in my role, I have read all kind of newspapers, major magazines, and literary works of this age. My primary concern is the theme, and I am a purist, appreciating genuine art for its own sake.

CITIZEN K: It's government-manufactured literature you appreciate— not art for art's sake.

INTERROGATOR: I like the works of Kim So-Weol and Seo Jung-Ju, because they give me a comfortable, peaceful feeling without making a big fuss. In a way, Kim Ji-Ha is writing worthless poetry.

CITIZEN K: You are one the conservative old-guard.

INTERROGATOR: Yes, I am. The investigator role I took represents ultra right-wing intellectuals.

CITIZEN K: How about we drop it for now and get back to the play?

INTERROGATOR: Please bear in mind that the exercise of overwhelming force is also an appropriately targeted strategy for treating those from the learned classes, which means, tell me the truth without killing any more time!.

CITIZEN K: Oh, shut up! The play must go on, as the script says.

(ACTOR A/INTERROGATOR *lightly touches* CITIZEN K*'s shoulder.* CITIZEN K *returns to the action of the play.*)

INTERROGATOR: Why are you covering up? Don't you have any confidence in what you did.

CITIZEN K: I've never gone against the law, never promulgated any kind of subversive treatises against your government. I've simply argued that justice in our age should not be solely your dominion. With a citizen's right, I declared that we should have freedom of speech. Why should that act violate the law?

INTERROGATOR: I am not sitting here to argue with you. *(Pulling an anthology of poetry out of some papers.)* Did you publish this anthology entitled, *For Us, There Is another Government*?

CITIZEN K: Yes I did.

INTERROGATOR: Where should that government should be built? On Yul Island?[14] How many people does it have? How big is it?

CITIZEN K: It would be a kind of free city-state built from my imagination, with no people and no territory.

INTERROGATOR: An anarchistic fantasy created from your dreams while sipping coffee in your study—do you realize the harm it could do to our society? *(Thumbing through the anthology.)* What kind of perverted word-play is this? *(Reads carefully.)* "Have you, on some day, some month, some year, been arrested for streaking on the Chung-Sa-Po beach by the Hae-Wun-Dae police and received an immediate trial ?"[15]

CITIZEN K: That's the way I write, the way I express myself. That's not real, however. Don't harass me for the poetic language that pops up in my imagination!

INTERROGATOR: Do you hang around the city every night, wearing pajamas and riding a motorbike?

CITIZEN K: That's my customary way of taking a stroll.

INTERROGATOR: Stupid bastard! Are you a pervert? *(Skimming quickly through the anthology.)* Did you ever piss in the DMZ?[16]

CITIZEN K: Pardon?

INTERROGATOR: Did you ever challenge Earnest Hemingway to a boxing match?

CITIZEN K: Yes!

INTERROGATOR: Have you ever seduced a runaway woman under a street light?

CITIZEN K: I seduce men, too!

INTERROGATOR: During the night, do you have the habit of calling someone for phone sex ?

CITIZEN K: Every night I call someone I want to meet under any terms. Yes, I am shamelessly corrupt. Punish me!

ACTOR A/INTERROGATOR: *Statement of the Ultra Right-Wing Intellectual*: Do you think that I could not figure out the meanings behind all the word-play? Now, let's proceed to Part 2: *At Last, Citizens Begin to Throw Stones.* This is the first line of your poem in the series, *Waiting for the Early Morning Newspaper.* "Editor's comments say, 'cut twelve lines.' Should I leave them blank? The disputants are sleeping now, and the light is on the telex room only. The telex machine alone clatters, pouring forth the shouts of demonstrations from the Philippines across the sea." It's interesting, "pouring forth the shouts of demonstrations." *(Pause.)* The title of this poem is quite Romantic: *The Free Port of the South Sea, Even Though I Do Not Know Thee.* But the contents are a perfect jumble. They try to foment revolution spontaneously, through their own energy.
"Mr. Aquinan, an acting section chief at the Manila National Bank, gleefully throws beer bottles into the street with Miss Marchè, a female staff member, the bottles smashing into foreheads of riot police who had entered the side street at the base of the building, and the department head who brings some rocks by elevator approaches the area of the windows with them in his hands. Throw it, throw!" . . . . It's chaos! Why is an acting section chief at the Manila National Bank throwing stones? Is this a poem? Is it supposed to be interesting? Look, Mr. Poet—we authorities don't care about this kind of agitated poem; it's meaningless. We don't care about rock-throwing demonstrations; they're like gnats trying to bring down an elephant.[17] We have our own way. Indirect agitation is no big deal, understand? Indirect agitation is so weak that you may say as much as you wish. Who cares? But why did you leaflet the manifesto, you son-of-a-bitch? *(Knocking K down and pressing on his forehead with his boots.)* What? "Let's get out of here without any hard feelings? When we meet out on the street by chance, we may go to a bar for a drink together"? Am I your friend? *(He slaps K's face.)* You are a shallow

wobbler, leaning whichever way the wind blows you! While I was going through hard times as a platoon leader, searching for the enemy crawling though the weed fields at the DMZ, you wrote a poem about taking a piss in the DMZ! And then what? *For Us, There Is Another Government.* You, you son-of-a-bitch, were demonstrating against the government, spending your parents' money well away from the front, south of the Han-Tan river, at the very same time that the enemy was cutting our soldiers' throats! While our pricks were frozen in the field by temperatures down to −30,[18] you went streaking in the street. Get undressed, you bastard, let's see how big your cock is. *(He kicks K in the groin. K screams.)* Human trash like you should be killed with an M-60![19] But, you scum, as I said, no matter what you did, I let it pass. Just write poems about masturbation and leave things alone. Do not leaflet any manifestos or anything like that. What! "A reporter's special morality." Someone will be crazy enough to give you a bonus for that. Right, you idiot! Great, make my day. For last three years, while I was doing hard time in the military, I loathed your kind. This is your last day, Ahaaaak! *(ACTOR A strikes K viciously.)*

CITIZEN K: Sir, sir, how can you treat me like this? *(ACTOR A strikes him more viciously.)*

CITIZEN K: What is this for? *(ACTOR A strikes fanatically, again and again.)*

CITIZEN K: Siiiiiir! You should not do this. *(ACTOR A stops with sneer.)*

INTERROGATOR: *(To the light booth.)* Take them out.

Light board operator, who is frightened, takes out the lights.

EPISODE 3. TORTURE

Scene shifts with a rising banging sound. A structure of a "prison within a prison" is created by a metallic image which separates the stage from the auditorium seats. In other words, the separation between stage and auditorium should be prominent. With some kind of electrical sound, black-lights turn on. There are crimson lines winding around the bodies of ACTOR B and of ACTOR C. Protracted staccato screams are projected onto the stage.
ACTORS B and C's choreography of despair.
Without any physical contact with the prisoners, the unseen torturers conduct their business by moving switches on and off.

As sparks sputter from her body, ACTOR B *screams.*
Like ACTOR B, ACTOR C *sobs.*
Enter CITIZEN K.

CITIZEN K: *(To the torturers.)* Stop it! What kind of savagery is this?

ACTOR C: *(To* CITIZEN K.*)* You son-of-a-bitch! Because you squealed
   to the police, we're suffering here. You snitched on those who signed
   the manifesto—you told the police!

CITIZEN K: No, for heaven's sake, I didn't!

ACTOR B: Is this what you wanted? Did you want to live on easy street.
   I can't believe that you're a traitor!

CITIZEN K: There's some mistake! Something gone wrong . . . .

ACTOR C: You turncoat! Did you think that you could live by yourself
   in this world?

CITIZEN K: I'm innocent! I'm not under suspicion!

ACTOR B: For long time, you have been an informer in the company.
   It's clear now why you didn't escape, but waited to be arrested without any resistance.

ACTOR C: You're garbage!

ACTOR B: Pig!

CITIZEN K: It's chaos, dreadful chaos. . .

ACTOR A/INTERROGATOR: *(Who may have been one of the torturers.)* Don't worry about it!

CITIZEN K: What! "Don't worry"?

INTERROGATOR: You're protected by the government.

CITIZEN K: What are you talking about?!

INTERROGATOR: I said, "don't worry." The signers will never get out
   of here. Period.

CITIZEN K: Hey, hey you, please get me out of here!

ACTOR C: Hey traitor, where are you going?!

ACTOR B: You're human garbage with no concern for our people or our
   nation!

CITIZEN K: Go on and hit me, hit me! You're slandering an innocent
   man.

The stage brightens suddenly, and all freeze in place.

INTERROGATOR: *(To the audience, explaining the government's way of
   controlling the mass media.)* As you see, these so-called intellectuals are
   split into factions just like that. With some simple tricks, they turn on
   each other. To split them into several factions is the key point. The wall

should first be cracked inside before it is struck from the outside. This is a truth proven by history. Yes, it is. Our strategy to counter-attack the mass media comes from this truth: first of all, make the readers turn their backs on the publishers, and then control the struggle inside, which leads the media to collapse by themselves. We followed the model of Goebbles, a German genius in anti-mass media strategy, which always needs some scapegoat. The scapegoat we chose was Citizen K.

The actors on stage unfreeze.
On the table is placed a spoon and boiled rice stew.
An interrogator contends with CITIZEN K.

ACTOR A/INTERROGATOR: Help yourself.
CITIZEN K: . . .
INTERROGATOR: Help yourself, I said.

Pause.

CITIZEN K: I'm not a traitor. *(Pause.)* You know that.
INTERROGATOR: Please understand me.
CITIZEN K: How could you let something like this happen?
INTERROGATOR: It's all a scenario I created. I know about the type-writer you used, and your signature is on the manifesto. That's all. I simply made some copies of the report you made for us, and showed them to your colleagues. Of course, since our sources reported every-day, at the very moment of the manifesto signing, I knew the internal situation at the company better than anyone else.
CITIZEN K: Why was I selected for this dirty job?
INTERROGATOR: You were recommended by our source. And I agreed with it, too. You neither actively participated in the company's internal strife, nor toadied up to your boss. You seemed to take an equivocal attitude. This vacillating side of your personality is a basic condition for informants, right? No one is on your side.
CITIZEN K: If you say so. . .
INTERROGATOR: You've got to understand me. Didn't you say, "once one is totally absorbed in his job, he might harm others regardless of his intentions"?
CITIZEN K: I understand you, all right. Your kind of son-of-a-bitch is very useful in this barbaric age.
INTERROGATOR: *(Pause.)* You probably don't know how powerful that electric chair is. It wastes men's minds

CITIZEN K: I'm already wasted.

INTERROGATOR: Your part is finished. *(Patting* CITIZEN K*'s shoulder.)* You may go home.

CITIZEN K: Where should I go, for Christ's sake?

INTERROGATOR: Go back home and resume your normal duties. You are free to walk the streets during the day. Your civilian rights are restored.

CITIZEN K: But my right to a livelihood was already taken.

INTERROGATOR: You're assigned as a reporter in the Culture Department of the newly merged newspaper company. Of course, I will not ask you to be an inside source for our government. Please regard this as thoughtful concern for you with no conditions attached by the government.

CITIZEN K: They shouldn't require conditions of me any more. I will be seen forever as a traitor who sold my colleagues down the river. You counted on that, too. Your source will report anonymously what's going on in the company, never revealing his identity, and I will be glared at like a leper. The internal situation in the company will become increasingly divisive, inviting a state of chaos. . .

INTERROGATOR: Once you get out of here, you'll have lost nothing, in fact. Presumably you may have some bad memories and some wounded pride, but they have nothing to do with your making a living.

CITIZEN K: *(Deciding to resist.)* You made a big mistake in destroying me. *(Pause.)* Yes, it is natural for the humble intellectuals to crumble in the face of physical violence. And, among them, an indecisive egocentric like me would want to give in to it. When I was first interrogated by you, my only hope was to be locked up unharmed in a prison cell. We reporters already knew that you beat us for no reason just to drive us out of our minds. You have a clear motive. You believe that physical violence is the only method to discourage writers who criticize the world with their tongues and pens. The critical reporter whose back becomes hardened from torture can no longer wield the power of the pen, and the chief editor who every morning brushes dentures where teeth used to be will be much more faithful to self-censorship. Keeping these desperate situations in mind, we began our career as reporters. There was a kind of a terror, a living threat we encountered every day. We had no choice but to be tamed. *(Pause.)* Yes. I lived such desperate moments. I was scared. It was probably during the first interrogation, I made up my mind to be a stoolpigeon for you. When you beat me up, I called you "sir". "Sir, how could you treat me like this?". . . "How could you?". . . "You are not supposed to do this!" I begged you clinging to your pants. At that time, you sneered at me.

INTERROGATOR: We think of this place as a kind of classroom. Something like the Non-San Military Training Center,[20] though the comparison may not be precise. We have some justification for doing this job in our own way, you know.

CITIZEN K: Justification for destroying intellectuals?

INTERROGATOR: No. It's a matter of controlling them through a system. In other words, we rebuild them as intellectuals who can contribute to the people of the nation, one body moving in one direction.

CITIZEN K: That sounds like totalitarianism.

INTERROGATOR: Don't you think that it's not good for our country to have so much haggling? That's the whole idea for this revision of the mass-media structure. The violence against you, malicious propaganda, strategies for internal divisiveness, etc.—all of these are inevitable choices in rebuilding a better country. So I ask your cooperation. You've got to trust me.

CITIZEN K: How can a weakling, a coward like me interfere with your policies? I am ashamed of myself for this. I would like to keep doing my job without bucking the tide. I really want to live without any trouble because of politics!

INTERROGATOR: Go back home. You have a choice.

CITIZEN K: I can't return home like this! It's not necessary to ruin me, a nobody. Why are you trying to force me into giving up my humanity?

INTERROGATOR: You must understand me!

CITIZEN K: "Understand you!" I begin to understand you all too clearly. Thus, *(Pause.)* I choose to resist.

INTERROGATOR: Please bear in mind that we could eliminate you if we wanted to.

CITIZEN K: I'm not going to go back to any position you arrange for me. As a citizen, I will denounce your violence and plots.

Pause.

INTERROGATOR: Break him into pieces!

Enter a TORTURER *(ACTOR C).*
CITIZEN K *is stripped naked.*
A rope of crimson color winds around K'S body.
The radio volume increases to the maximum.

CITIZEN K: *(Quoting words of Mr. Kim Keun-Tae, a repressed politician.)* "You seat us in the torture chair; however, someday you will be seated in the chair of justice of democratic citizens."[21]

TORTURER: *(Quoting the words of Lieutenant Lee Keun Ahn, a professional torturer.)* "It's my turn now, and when the democratic country you dream of evolves, I am willing to sit down in that chair. And then it will be your turn."[22]

With CITIZEN K*'s gruesome scream—Black out.*

EPISODE 4. IDEOLOGICAL STRUGGLE— IN THE PRISON CELL

The setup of the prison cell is like a hospital room. The room in which some prisoners (or patients) lounge holding i.v. bottles looks beautiful with colorful lights of blue and orange. It is somehow strange that, in Episode 4, the most disgusting and sickest confined place is dressed-up with a colorful light design. It's true that the mood of this scene is contrasted to the other scenes as if we are looking into a magic glass. This magic-glass-like-stage itself symbolizes a side of South Korean society.

Enter CITIZEN K.
Everyone glares at him.
Tension, and Silence.

ACTOR A: *(From the dark.)* What political stance?

ACTOR B: *(From the dark.)* Extremely left-wing?

ACTOR C: *(From the dark.)* Extremely right-wing?

ACTOR A: *(From the dark.)* Or somewhere in the middle of the left?

ACTOR B: *(From the dark.)* Somewhere in the middle of the right?

ACTOR C: *(From the dark.)* This guy seems to me a middle-of-the-roader after all.

CITIZEN K: No, I am a free citizen! What am I here for?

ACTOR C: *(In the dark.)* You're denounced!

CITIZEN K: What do you mean, "denounced"?

Lights up on the stage.

ACTOR A: *(This man plays an* EX-INSPECTOR GENERAL/ASSASSIN *in this scene.)* Your name is Kim Yo-Seop, isn't it?

CITIZEN K: How do you know my na . . . .

ACTOR A/ASSASSIN: My lawyer team was just talking about you.
You're the first fingered and arrested among the intellectuals who
signed the manifesto. I am still in touch with your organization. Welcome, colleague.

CITIZEN K: You are. . .?

ASSASSIN: I was a general director of the secret information agency.
Do you remember that gunshot fired in April this year? That was me.
I missed the target, but I demonstrated that there is a power of con-
science opposed to the dictatorship in our bureaucratic society.

ACTOR D/SINGER: *(This girl is a singer who sells her body to the
powerful.)* I am a singer. You've got attractive eyes.

ASSASSIN: Bitch. Ignore her. That girl sleeps around with politicians.
Even here in the prison cell, she can't change her ways and she's still
a whore. . . .

SINGER Who the fuck are you talking to? Until last year you leeched
off the money which we earned by selling ourselves. You're a patriot?
No way. You can't pull the wool over our eyes! We all knew that you
were forced into a tight spot and fired!

ASSASSIN: Shut up! You stupid bitch! What do you know?

SINGER: *(To K.)* I hoped that this world would be better place for me to
live even though I used to sell my body. Now, this world is rotten to
the core. I heard from somebody that the power of conscience like
yours would build a free country, opening these bars. Come on! Please
show me a world where girls like me will be treated like human beings.

A sharp whistle.
A prison guard is suspended in space

SINGER: That son-of-a-bitch. *(To K.)* He's calling me. I like you. See
you in a while.

ACTOR D *goes to the black curtain upstage while waving lightly,
then shows a brief smile before she goes behind the curtain to the
judge who summoned her.*

CITIZEN K: Damn it! Even this special judge is corrupted!

ACTOR A's *Narration of an Assassin*: They're screwing everyday. Life
here stinks! *(Staring behind the black curtain.)* I should eliminate that
son-of-a-bitch, but I can't. Bribing the powers that be with sex and
money, that grafter became their right-hand man. I was always a left-

hand man. I took care of all his messy business for him, but I didn't benefit from it at all. But, that worm has . . . *(Pause.)* There is no one but you, a political fighter, who can get rid of him.

CITIZEN K: Someone like me. Why?

ASSASSIN: Because the intellectuals like you who signed the manifesto have tremendous support from the public

CITIZEN K: I am a just an ordinary guy. I have no interest in power games.

ASSASSIN: It's fine with me if you don't trust me. This country is the great bust of our age. I've never heard of a government that had such sweeping power, and a system of law as corrupt as this is unprecedented. All of which resulted from a mysterious political system over the last eighteen years. Every law and rule is a forgery, all governmental departments and officers are merely puppets. They don't know where the power comes from that commands, promotes, and liquidates their very selves. The very center of the power is shown to them as a mysterious and unavoidable shadow of a fortress. Haven't you seen it?! The guard who is supposed to watch this fortress is accustomed to bribes of money and sex. And the old guy like me holding some dream of revolution is helplessly terminated.

CITIZEN K: Then, the judge himself must be corrupted by that power.

ASSASSIN: Now, it's time to bring that castle down. I couldn't do this job alone, pruning rotten branches with my own hands. It's your turn. I am begging you, the leader of the anti-regime civilian intelligentsia.

CITIZEN K: I'm not a revolutionary.

ACTOR B/FEMALE COLLEGE STUDENT: You're a hypocrite!

ASSASSIN: College students these days are aggressive.

ACTOR B'S *Narration of the Female Leader of Student Power*: You forget the fact that you share in the tarnishing of this world through inequity and corruption. We militant activists and laborers now condemn your pseudo-efforts to realize a just society. You're simply a loser discarded by corrupt power. Don't you know better than anyone else that your behavior cannot be rationalized with some theory?

ACTOR A/ASSASSIN: When I was a college student, I was intoxicated with dreams of revolution—like you. But you should not be under the illusion that everything will be solved by your immature demonstration. Someday, you will recognize that the theories you argued are merely pipe dreams.

COLLEGE STUDENT: It may be true for your kind of persons who are accustomed to accepting orders, to compromise and obedience. But perhaps you feel the force of the revolutionary flame now growing. You are betting on this ploy to get in on this new power, aren't you?

CITIZEN K: It is not fair to abuse an individual using an extreme theory of some national crisis!

COLLEGE STUDENT: You know that you're at best an opportunist. "An extreme theory"? This is why you intellectuals noncommittally wobble, blown from this side to that, keeping your head down to live a safe life.

CITIZEN K: Practical morality cannot exist disregarding reality.

COLLEGE STUDENT: What have you done about this fucked-up world except mouth sophistry about justice and freedom, and sell your knowledge to feed your empty stomach? Where can we find any meaning in your revolutionary theories concocted around some table, and how potent do you think they may be? You just walked in here by yourself as if you were trying to prove that you were clean. Isn't it true that you're using this prison cell as a place of refuge?

SINGER *(Entering from behind the curtain while rearranging her disheveled dress. To the* JUDGE.*)* Son-of-a-bitch! You're sick of me, aren't you?

CITIZEN K: *(Replying to* ACTOR B/COLLEGE STUDENT.*)* I am very tired and not in the mood to discuss it with you.

ACTOR D'S *Narration by a Singer-Prostitute, Who Calls Citizen K the "Last Hope"*: *(To the others.)* Hey, it's okay with me that you're talking about revolution and demonstration, but leave him alone. He is our last hope, you know? *(Hugging* CITIZEN K.*)* Are you tired? You look pale. Don't worry. Everyone who comes here has the same problem at first. Most of the prisoners are high-strung. But I'm here. I'll take care of you.

CITIZEN K: *(Shoves the* SINGER *in the face, thrusting her away from him.)*

SINGER: Why are you pushing me around? Ah, I get it. Because I'm a whore? Son-of-a-bitch. Right, I'm doing a dirty job, but how clean are your jobs? Hypocrites! Cowards! Your façade looks good, but you're supposed to be hanged, just like me.

COLLEGE STUDENT: Don't torture yourself. We must fight on until the day of freedom is come. We citizens must build the democratic history by ourselves fighting today's conflicts. We citizens ourselves must bring to reality a democratic history through today's discord and conflict. Come on, keep your spirits up! Nothing is settled yet.

SINGER: Leave me alone! How come everybody is so smart? What is a citizen? I don't care anything about revolution and demonstrations.

But when you get fucked with a messy, disgusting dick, then you have a right to discuss affairs of the world. Understand? You, cock-suckers!

CITIZEN K: Anybody there? Get a move on! Begin the trial!

ACTOR B: "A trial"? You want to get a trial? You're crazy as a loon to submit to the authority of the old judiciary system. I cannot stomach a kind of trial which obscures the truth and encourages chaos. *(Toward ACTOR C who has just entered as a JAILOR.)* I deny the authority of any law over me.

JAILOR/ACTOR C *breaks an i.v. bottle attached to* ACTOR B/ COLLEGE STUDENT *and takes her out.*

EPISODE 5. IDEOLOGICAL STRUGGLE—AT THE TRIAL

The stage is decorated with lines symbolizing a power structure in which the totalitarian order dominates. Woven of a metallic construction in which the horizontal lines imply people of all classes and the vertical lines imply social rank. Between the seats in the auditorium and the stage there is a certain feeling of despair. With the sound of the percussion which begins at the end of Scene 4, the stage setting is changed in sections. The percussive sound of metallic friction during the scene shift naturally becomes a sound effect. The seat for the JUDGE/ACTOR A is green in this scene.

Enter CITIZEN K *from the auditorium.*
He sits in the chair positioned between the stage and the auditorium.
A strong light is switched on, illuminating his front.

CITIZEN K: Turn out the light!

ACTOR A/JUDGE: Why? Are you ashamed to be seen because your body is trembling with guilt?

CITIZEN K: Why do you obscure yourself?

JUDGE: I am sitting here in front of you. Look at me. No self-confidence? What are you afraid of? I am a leader in the justice of our times.

CITIZEN K: The justice of our times does not belong to you. Let's discuss it when we're both on equal footing.

JUDGE: The justice of our age is not a subject for debate. It's a practice and a movement. You're still besotted with opium-like knowledge. I did not apprehend you to discuss justice with me, but for you to reflect on what you have done, and to give you a second chance for rehabilitation.

CITIZEN K: Turn out that light! I will stand trial staring at your eyes. Do not camouflage yourself with these gimmicks.

JUDGE: "Gimmicks"? How dare you utter that word from your filthy mouth? You manipulated the students out into the street with your glib tongue, and made them throw stones and flame-bottles at us. You incited laborers with worthless theories, and aided and abetted yourself right out of work.

CITIZEN K: That is a conflict in life choices they sort out for themselves.

(The interrogation light is turned out and the audience now can see the judge.)

JUDGE: *(Who has the right to conduct legal coercion.)* You now vindicate students and laborers who choose violent struggle as a right to live. I aver that my legal dominance is necessary to secure justice in our age.

CITIZEN K: Your theory drives conflict between us as a nation.

JUDGE: Our society is descending into chaos. Irresponsible intellectuals are to blame for it.

CITIZEN K: No, your fascist government is to blame.

JUDGE: *(In his practical view.)* The revolutionary cabinet has done a remarkable job of developing this country, overcoming remnants of the colonial system and resolving the problem of famine in the chaos of independence. You are comfortably fed and clothed, and your housing has been remarkably upgraded. You have nothing to complain about when you think of the food you eat, clothes you wear, and the traffic system you use everyday.

CITZEN K: Those things are not benefits you created. They are merely relief baubles which you got from a super power country as a reward for giving up our independence.[23] You turn the general public into pigs with worthless relief *matériel*.

JUDGE: Are you a truly hungry Diogenes? Did you eat not for yourself, but for the public? Did you go to college, and get a diploma, and get a job for the public? Are you living not for yourself, but for the public?

CITIZEN K: I am . . .

JUDGE: It is for yourself, for your proud knowledge, that you are living.

CITIZEN K: I am in anguish!

JUDGE: "Anguish"? For whom?

CITIZEN K: For myself, ... and for our neighbors . . . .

JUDGE: "Neighbors"? Who are your neighbors? Are they real things?

CITIZEN K: My colleagues, my literature, college students who are waiting for a trial and here, *(To the auditorium.)* our neighbors in here. . . . .

JUDGE: Stop begging for their sympathy with your two-faced demagoguery!

CITIZEN K: *(A Statement for a Trial.)* And for you! *(Pause.)* I anguish for you, Your Honor. My anguish is a very tiny, simple one. I recognized that the greater the learning, the greater the sickness. Yes. I am a learned man. I know my role well. Every morning I went to my office, and wrote down the events of the day before and edited them to fit into a column. Reading and criticizing the day's events, we tried to suggest what's going to happen tomorrow. All these things, of course, happened at a desk. Do I have power? Does your knowledge have any power? No one knows. One of my colleagues condemned me for not participating in the struggle, students attacked us for fainthearted citizenship, and you government officials detain here in prison occasionally in order to tame us. Do I have power? *(Pause.)* When we asked ourselves, we would be mired in intense doubt. Do I have power? Yes. We are writing and talking at least. We believe that our opinions cannot offer the public any real food, but can suggest to them some power to choose for themselves by thinking rationally. Do not even try to deprive us of this function!

JUDGE: If you're a worthless daydreamer, rejected even by your peers, what then?

CITIZEN K: No, that's not true. Believing that our society is still concerned with rational truth, I signed the manifesto with them.

JUDGE: Naïve dreamer! Since your dreams are so naïve, you should be expelled from this society forever without being spared the dishonor.

CITIZEN K: As an intellectual, it was my fair and proper right to sign the manifesto! Release me, if you're sane.

JUDGE: It was not us but your cohorts who denounced you to the authorities.

CITIZENK: What?!

JUDGE: Bring the witnesses in.

Enter ACTOR B *and* ACTOR C.

JUDGE: *(To* ACTOR C.*)* Did you denounce this man?

ACTOR C: *(Pause.)* Yes, I did.

JUDGE: When? How? Why?

ACTOR C *(one of K's colleagues) bears false witness.*

ACTOR C: It was two days before distributing the manifesto on free speech. We gathered in Kim Yo-Seop's apartment. He gave us the first draft of the manifesto, completed before we got there, and he gave us a concrete plan for distributing it.

JUDGE: Is Kim Yo-Seop a prime mover in this scheme?

ACTOR C: He was a senior reporter to us, and our spiritual leader.

JUDGE: So?

ACTOR C: I informed the authorities.

CITIZEN K: No, it's not true! That's a complete fabrication!

JUDGE: If you have a lawyer in this world who will speak in your defense, bring him in.

CITIZEN K: This trial is null and void! What that college girl said inside the prison was right! I should have rejected this lousy legal process.

JUDGE: Summon the next witness.

CITIZEN K: *(Looking at ACTOR B.)* She has nothing to do with my arrest. Please don't involve her.

JUDGE: She's already involved.

CITIZEN K: As a democratic citizen, I vow to tell nothing but the truth!

JUDGE: Kim Yo-Seop is arrested for subversive plotting of a socialist dictatorship, undermining the present democratic government. Does the witness agree with the charge against the accused?

FEMALE REPORTER: *(Even though she is in love with K, she perjures herself.)* I do.

JUDGE: Any reason?

FEMALE REPORTER: He forced us to accept things that were different from the original direction for the freedom of speech manifesto. We signed reluctantly, and his subversive contents were inserted regardless of our opinion.

JUDGE: How did you make up your mind to stand before this court? Have you no pity for him you love?

FEMALE REPORTER: *(controlling her emotion)* I . . . think . . . that national security is more important . . . than . . . a personal love . . .

JUDGE: Thus, do you think he is guilty?

FEMALE REPORTER: Yes, he is!

CITIZEN K: Stop the trial!

Black out.
Gloomy interlude—a fugue.

EPISODE 6. EVERYDAY LIFE ITSELF WAS ARRESTED.

Again, a room in CITIZEN K*'s apartment.*

CITIZEN K: *(In soliloquy.)* Am I free now? Or, am I still in prison. Why did the judge release me? Is it a kind of generosity to a loser who is not much as an intellectual? If so, I am worthless trash not even fit to be punished. Yes, I am merely trash. Oh, how did they make her betray me? Or are they the true betrayers, they who inflated themselves with cheap heroism and a weak sense of justice, but who changed their colors when faced with the present oppression, hiding themselves behind a thick shell? *(Pause.)* Am I free now? Or am I still in prison? Why did the judge discharge me? Am I seen as an affable intellectual who caved into self-censorship? *(Pause.)* Right, the present itself is arrested. Don't forget this. *(Pause.)* I will go to work tomorrow morning as the arrested. I will keep doing my job in this arrested present situation. *(Pause.)* I must not stand back.

CITIZEN K *sits in front of the typewriter.*
A solemn requiem, mixing with the noise of typing.
Enter ACTOR A *with this music; he looks down at* CITIZEN K.
CITIZEN K. *returns the look.*
Crescendo requiem.
ACTOR A *takes a small hatchet out of his jacket.*
Music volume increases.
Flash! K's hand raises.
More solemn music!
Black out.

Epilogue

Empty room.
A clock strikes the time.
There are some books and a glass on the table, and
a morning newspaper delivered now. Under the light on the desk,
a clock keeps striking.
Leaving some materials of the learned man,
Where does he go?

-Finis-

NOTES:

1. Gwangju is the site of the infamous "Gwangju Incident," also called the "Gwangju Massacre," that occurred May 17–27, 1980, a civil uprising resulting from governmental abuses and which led to the deaths of hundreds of Korean civilians at the hands of crack armed forces. President Park Chung-Hee and his chief bodyguard, Cha Ji-Cheol, were assassinated by Kim Jae-Kyu at a private dinner in the Korean Central Intelligence Agency compound on October 26, 1979.

2. A popular South Korean song of the day.

3. The seemingly confused geography may be a metaphor for the confused state of affairs in South Korea at the time.

4. The *Gukje* and *Jayu* newspapers were influential anti-regime papers at the time.

5. 1.42 inches, 23°F. and 50°F., respectively.

6. A student leader, famous for anti-regime songs. A kind of Korean Bob Dylan then, now a director of the Hakcheon theatre company in Seoul.

7. Oh Jang-Hwan was a left-wing poet and literary leader who went to live in North Korea in 1948. His works reflect the enforced subjugation of Korean heritage and culture during the Japanese colonial period 1910–1945.

8. 4.19 refers to the April 19, 1960 student uprising in protest against the regime of President Rhee Syngman, protests that resulted in the death and injury of many students, but which ultimately helped to topple Rhee's government. April 19 is still an important day of commemoration in South Korea.

9. The Korean language script refers to mask dance plays *(talchum)* popular in Korea. During the period prior to the twentieth century, the plays were staged at important times in the lunar year. Common folk played the roles in masks, satirically criticizing the landowners, nobility, and monks who normally could not be so criticized by the lower classes. The upper classes, it is said, put up with the infrequent satires in order to give the lower classes a way to release their frustrations and ill-feelings toward the upper classes. The Korean language reference is so steeped in Korean culture that it is impossible to translate effectively in a few words.

10. Clear distilled spirits (often cheap) much favored by Korean men.

11. Poetry is a popular literary form in Korea, long used as a weapon of protest against forces of oppression. Seo Jung-Ju (pseudonym: Midang) is perhaps the most important Korean poet of the late twentieth century, first published in 1941. Some commentators note a parallel between his career and that of the Irish poet, Yeats. Kim Chun-Su was a prolific writer of symbolist work. During the 1970s and 1980s, he experimented with "non-meaning theory" in an attempt to free his poems of all conceptualizations. Kim Su-Yeong was taken by Communist forces in 1950, then freed by U.N. forces, but spent time in a P.O.W. camp until 1953. He was deeply affected by the April 19, 1960 protests. He was hit by a bus and died in 1968. Kim Ji-Ha was a dedicated fighter of the Park Chun-Hee regime. He was imprisoned, sentenced to death, but freed eight years later, released in 1980. Kim So-Weol (pseudonym: Kim Cheong-sik) was a celebrated, popular poet whose work often focused on a beloved, a lost home, or the unattainable. His "folksong style" words were often put to music. He committed suicide in 1934, at the age of 32.

12. The text of the poem, anonymously translated, is this:

Until I spoke his name,
He had been
no more than a mere gesture.
When I spoke his name,
one fitting this color and odor of mine,
as I spoke his name,
so that I may go to him
and become his flower.
We all wish
to become something.
You to me and I to you
wish to become an unforgettable gaze.

13. *Five Enemies* was written by Kim Ji-Ha in 1970. Accused of violating the National Security Law, he was imprisoned. The five enemies are: corporate conglomerates (*chaebol*), members of the National Assembly, high ranking government officials, military generals, and government ministers. The book was banned until 1984. (Thanks to Kim Alyssa for her input here.)

14. Yul Island (Yul-do) is an imaginary place; the literal meaning is "Chestnut Island." The island is mentioned in Korea's most famous ancient novel, *The Tale of Hong Gil-Dong*, written by Heo Gyun (1569–1618).

15. A famous beach in Busan, on the southeast tip of the Korean peninsula. Lee Yun-Taek hails from Busan.

16. An artificial buffer created in 1953 between North and South Korea, about three miles wide and 150 miles long along which thousands of North Korean troops on one side and South Korean and American soldiers on the other continue in a state of heightened readiness. The DMZ also happens to be one of Asia's premier wildlife sanctuaries, having been a "no-man's land" for over 50 years.

17. The Korean script equates rocks and eggs in complicated imagery.

18. −22°F.

19. A medium machine gun used by military crews, especially on helicopters.

20. A place where all military recruits go through boot camp.

21. An anti-regime leader at that time and former administrator of the Bureau of Social Care. He was subjected to water and electric torture in 1985 at the hands of the torturer, Lee Keun-Ahn, whom he later forgave.

22. The most notorious torturer during the military regime. Lee Keun-Ahn favored dislocating limbs, jolting with electricity, and pouring pepper-laced water into his victims' noses. He was decorated sixteen times for service to the government, but went into hiding after political prisoners were released in 1988 and a more open government instituted. He surrendered in 1999 and was sentenced to seven years imprisonment.

23. Lee clearly refers to the United States here.

Introduction to *O-Gu:*
A Ceremony of Death

O-Gu: A Ceremony of Death is the first of Lee Yun-Taek's works that experienced wide-spread commercial success and critical acclaim. First produced in 1989, the initial production was directed by Chae Yun-Il, with Lee assuming direction the following year. It was in 1997, when the popular "grandmotherly" soap opera actress, Kang Bu-Ja, joined the cast that audiences flocked to performances. Now, an estimated 2.7 million have seen the various incarnations of the play, the most recent in July 2006. *O-Gu* has become a "classic" modern Korean play, but the Western reader will recognize the cheapskate older son, the conniving younger son, the unhappy daughter-in-law, the sexy widow, botched rituals, inept beings from the Other World, cheating at cards and other human foibles and universal truths that surpass cultural boundaries.

Though the play's subtitle is *A Ceremony of Death*, *O-Gu* is the most life affirming play of the four in this anthology. An aged mother has visions of death in her sleep and urges her eldest son to pay for a shaman ceremony to prepare the way for her death and reunion with her long-deceased husband. The son, who doesn't want to spend money for a shaman, tries to put her off, but she will not be dissuaded and the ceremony is arranged and staged. At a climactic moment in it, the mother in fact dies and the dramatic action of remainder of the play takes us through what the Irish call "the wake" and the subsequent arrival of three Messengers from the Other World who come to claim the deceased mother.

The structure of the play displays Lee Yun-Taek's theatrical ingenuity. Shamanistic rites *(kut)* may be the proto-typical Korean theatre form, combining as they do music, dance, singing, chanting, costume changes, trance, quasi-magic, dialogue between spirits and the shaman, and audience participation. Despite Korea's urbanity and large Christian population, shamans are commonly consulted during family crises or illnesses, so Lee consciously and creatively employed rites theatrical in and of themselves and an accepted aspect of Korean culture. "*O-Gu*" is a word Lee created, but the shamanistic rites in the play are based on those from around the Busan area where Lee grew up. A song ("let's enjoy, let's enjoy while we are young") sung in act one by the Female Shaman is a drinking song well known across Korea. Through such use of folk music, Lee's quest for a "populist" theatre is manifest.

As the play unfolds, a variety of rites become vehicles for theatrical experiences. The rites invite some mourners to sing, others to dance, two social activities much-beloved by Koreans. Moreover, the preparation of the corpse, dressing it in a particular order and fashion, behavior of the eldest son and chief mourner, even the food to be consumed—such rites are used by Lee engage sentimental feelings, which often are quickly followed by broad comedy bringing knowing smiles or broad guffaws. But Lee's special instinct for theatre is most evidenced when he brings the deceased mother to life in order to rebuke her sons, who were already dividing up her property before her death, but her "tongue-lashing" is delivered through her angry mime, rather than words, interpreted by one Messenger from the Other World.

A card game called "Chun Doo-Whan Go-Stop" is a highly visible part of Korean life, played in parks, at small tables outside of small convenience stores, and through the second act of *O-Gu*. It is a device through which Lee exposes the darker side of human cupidity and sexual desire at the same time he comically exposes those same qualities in the Messengers from the Other World. The Eldest Son is crazed in his need to win all the money and one Messenger from the Other World has yearnings for the widow that clearly are of this world. But, Lee's dramaturgical control is certain and un-erring. Balancing humor (life) in the presence of death and darker urges even in the lighter moments of life, he visualizes for us one of the play's central themes, stated by Seok-Chul, the shaman at the close of the play: "People, don't be saddened by thoughts of the Other World, but enjoy the time of your life, performing a *kut* as an homage to it. Then, without fear, let's go there [to the Other World] together."

It is interesting that *O-Gu* is the only play in the anthology that consistently uses character names—that is, characters are defined by name and not by function. Even one of the Messengers from the Other World has a given name. The use of names suggests personalization in characterizations and, indeed, the quality of each character's dialogue is clearly different from the others, as the touching scene near the play's conclusion suggests. The granddaughter, Bong-Suk, asks:

BONG-SUK: Where are you taking my grandma?

MESSENGER 3: To my grandpa.

BONG-SUK: *Your* grandpa?

MESSENGER 3: Yes.

BONG-SUK: Who is your grandpa? Yama? The King of the Underworld?

MESSENGER 3: Hee heee. Everybody calls him the King of the Underworld?

BONG-SUK Mmmm. What's his name?

MESSENGER 3: Young people aren't much use these days. They forget their own grandpa's name.

BONG-SUK: That's because he died years ago. I never see him. *(Pause as she thinks.)* Got it! It's In Seok-Choe.

MESSENGER 3: That's the same name as my grandpa.

BONG-SUK: You mean that's two men with same name?

MESSENGER 3: No, that's the same person.

BONG-SUK: Wow. . .so you mean my grandma is supposed to meet my grandpa?

MESSENGER 3: You might say that.

BONG-SUK: I wish I could go with her.

MESSENGER 3: Don't bother; you'll be there some day, sooner or later.

BONG-SUK: Where is "there," anyway? Is it really far away?

MESSENGER 3: No, it's very near here.

BONG-SUK: Very near? Where?

MESSENGER 3: *(Poking her breast.)* Right here!

BONG-SUK: *(Frowns at him a little.)* You're strange.

MESSENGER 3: *(Embarrassed.)* No, I don't mean . . . .

BONG-SUK: To touch a lady's breast like that. . .

MESSENGER 3: I'm only telling you the truth!

BONG-SUK: Truth?

MESSENGER 3: Yeah, we are neither sent here by Yama nor going back to the Other World by taking Korean Air Lines. I was born out of your mind. I mean that I was born out of the imagination of human beings. Therefore, we're all one body and one spirit.

BONG-SUK: *(Tenderly taking* MESSENGER *3's hand.)* You're right. We're all one spirit and one feeling because we are performing a play now.

Lee's 2003 film version of his play, titled *O-Gu: Hilarious Mourning*, received lukewarm critical response and was a box-office disappointment. No single reason seems to explain the results: Lee suggests he tried to do too much with the film. I suggest that the film's subject matter probably did not appeal to the largely youthful film audiences and my own response to the film is that the screen writing often lacks the theatricality and truths inherent in the stage play.

Citizen K, *The Dummy Bride*, and *Mask of Fire* are plays about ideas or social issues. The generally one-dimensional characters who inhabit those plays function largely as symbols of good or evil, depravity or innocence, uprightness or ambivalence, etc. The clash of ideas or political stances is more important than multi-dimensional human qualities and, thus, the plays have intellectual heat, but are aesthetically cool, even distancing. Though the plays clearly are Korean, the ideas are conveyed by symbols of humanity, making adaptation for production in another culture not all that difficult.

O-Gu is the most humane and human of the plays in this anthology, perhaps because it is a play about people, not about ideas. Of course, *O-Gu* contains themes of import, but the play has great heart, great warmth. Characters never preach in the play and Lee lets the readers (audience members) take from the play what they will. The cultural specificity in *O-Gu* may require that it be staged only by someone deeply steeped in Korean culture, much as a *noh* or *kabuki* performed in English requires considerable knowledge of Japanese culture. However, there is much in *O-Gu* for the Western reader to enjoy.

O-Gu: A Ceremony of Death

Dramatis Personae:

Seok-Chul, a male shaman
A female shaman assistant
An aged mother
The first son
The second son
The first daughter-in-law
Bong-Suk, granddaughter of the aged mother
Messenger 1 from the Other World
Messenger 2 from the Other World
Messenger 3 from the Other World
A widow
Funeral guests *(double cast with Messenger 1, 2, and 3)*
Kim, an errand boy

PROLOGUE

An aged MOTHER *in her seventies is sleeping in her neat ramie cloth vest with a well-worn 108-bead Buddhist rosary in her hand. A traditional song sung by the elderly in the Busan area is playing. The* MOTHER *remains sleeping until the audience is seated.*

MOTHER: Ah . . . ahck *(She shouts, surprising the audience, and the house lights go out.)* Oh, gosh, almost got in trouble. Tagga! Tagga! *(Enter the* ELDEST SON, TAG, *in his fifties, in the shabby suit of an elementary school teacher. In a flattering voice.)* Tagga.

1ST SON: What's up?

MOTHER: I almost got into trouble.

1ST SON: *(Picking at his ear.)* Not again . . .

MOTHER: This time, I was got directly, not by the messengers from the Other World, but by the King of Hell himself.

1ST SON: *(Loudly.)* Yama[1] is coming to . . .

MOTHER: To ask me to go out with him.

(Pause)

1ST SON: Oh, boy! It's time you got a new line of stories!

(Pause.)

MOTHER: *(Girlishly.)* Dear Tag. . .

1ST SON: It's 'Taek', not 'Tag', you got it?

MOTHER: My pronunciation is from King Sejong's *Dictionary of Proper Korean Pronunciation!*[2]

1ST SON: Stop calling me, "Tagga, Tagga," please! I'm old enough to have a grandson, Mom.

MOTHER: *(Sulking.)* I'm on my way out . . .

1ST SON: *(Shouting towards the wings.)* Honey, would you give some cash to mom, please? She's going out to Pagoda Park[3] as usual. *(To* MOTHER.*)* Don't play Japanese cards for coins, Mom, please. It doesn't look good, those old people who play cards in the park.

MOTHER: Why, you little. . .

1ST SON: *(Snickering.)* I'm used to your empty threat that you'll move out with all your baggage.

MOTHER: *(Sullenly.)* I'm not joking.

1ST SON: How many times have you said that: "I'm not joking." ? You had me fooled until I was a junior high student still clutching your skirt when I fell.

(Pause.)

MOTHER: My empty threats are all used up.

1ST SON: Then, just lean on me as I say! I'm the eldest son in our family; I'll take care of you.

MOTHER: That's the way I want it to be, but they keep saying, "Let's go!"

1ST SON: Who says? Yama and the rest?

MOTHER: You got it.

1ST SON: Tell them to shut their mouths.

MOTHER: Please let me have a bang-up *kut* [4] performance.

1ST SON: *(Slapping his forehead.)* Good grief!

MOTHER: What's the matter with you? Huh? Don't you want me to go to heaven? Don't you?

1ST SON: Don't start again.

MOTHER: All right. You and your wife want me to fall into hell so that my unsaved soul shows up in your nightmare every single night. Is that what you want?

1ST SON: That's a superstition, I'm telling you.

MOTHER: Don't you have ancestors? You son-of-a-bitch!

1ST SON: What are you talking about? What's the relation between a ceremony for ancestors and performing a *kut* . . . ?

MOTHER: They're identical twins!

1ST SON: But, a *kut* costs money.

MOTHER: Who will be the owner of this house when I die . . .

1ST SON: Money is not the only subject here . . .

MOTHER: *(Starting to sob.)* Ever since your daddy was shot during the war, before he was thirty, I bought this house with my own money saved from selling rice cakes, and put two kids through school.

1ST SON: You're kidding. How could you buy a house selling rice cakes?

MOTHER: These days, no one shovels down rice cakes the way they used to because the cakes have a Western taste, but in the good old days, smart ass, there were many people who became rich selling them.

1ST SON: Watch your mouth, Mom, please. Don't forget I'm a school teacher whose mother should use decent language.

MOTHER: You'll have a bad mouth, too, when you're my age.

1ST SON: Okay. . . What do you say to a holiday trip in Southeast Asia? I'll give you my entire September bonus.

MOTHER: Why would I go to Southeast Asia?

1ST SON: Everybody has been there, these days.

MOTHER: Crazy bums! If they take their very last breath there, there will be no ceremony for their soul forever and ever!

1ST SON: You'd like the wonderful white beaches down there.

MOTHER: Do you *really* think I would enjoy swimming down there?

1ST SON: How about a sand poultice, then?

MOTHER: Just knock it off and call Seok-Chul.

1ST SON: Seok-Chul. . .What kind of dog's name is that? That son-of-bitch with his nose in the air, acting bigger than he is. . .

MOTHER: He is very busy lately.

1ST SON: Sure, that bum will buy high-rise buildings doing *kut* performances.

MOTHER: Stop calling him a bum. He has connections with King of Death.

1ST SON: It's not only the cost . . . .

MOTHER: Please just do what I say this time, while I'm still alive.

1ST SON: To be honest with you, the *kut* can be heard all over the village.

MOTHER: What are you talking about?

1ST SON: They beat gongs and drums, and dance with knives ...

MOTHER: That's interesting!

1ST SON: I'd be ashamed to be seen in the village if I held a *kut* performance for you, Mother.

MOTHER: You lollygagging bum! If holding a *kut* performance is embarrassing for you, why do people buy tickets to watch a *kut* performance these days?

1ST SON: Because the government has made it a culturally precious asset.[5]

MOTHER: Seok-Chul is a culturally precious asset himself. If you don't know it, just be quiet and pay the money to arrange a grand O-Gu *kut* performance for me.

1ST SON: How come the human cultural asset thing gets in on it?

MOTHER: The title doesn't matter. The shaman should be the center of the *kut* performance. That's what the shaman's for.

1ST SON: Let's play on!

ACT I

Kut—A Ceremonial Performance for a Living Death

A funerary beat is playing; the 1ST SON *and* HIS WIFE *are busily preparing the altar. The altar should be the Seongju style ceremonial table.[6] The aged* MOTHER *is sitting on her seat wearing "the garment for a living death," which looks very expensive. Enter a gong player, who places his instrument on a tripod made of three wooden sticks. A FE-MALE SHAMAN ASSISTANT, wearing a traditional garment for a male, attaches calligraphy to the* MOTHER's *back: "Long Live Mrs.*

Lee Bok-Nye." Holding a fan in her one hand, and a gourd water dipper and a handkerchief in the other, she takes her place against the altar, staring at the gong player. Now the kut performance is ready. . . .

SEOK-CHUL: *(Facing the stage audience and chanting.)* Mrs. Lee Bok-Nye who lost her husband during the Second World War, since that time on, has tried to survive with her two kids, going from place to place, selling such things as vegetables, rice cakes, meals, and clothing from a stall to have them educated.

MOTHER: I never sold meals from a stall.

SEOK-CHUL: You just said that, the other day, didn't you?

MOTHER: That's a story you made up. When did I tell you that? I think this *kut* may be the last chance for me, so let's cut the fictitious stories and get on with it.

SEOK-CHUL: All right, no problem. Not selling meals but selling rice cakes, little by little she saved enough money to buy a house abandoned by Japanese colonials, and some other realty, but now she is on the edge of her life, just in front of the stairway to heaven. Alas, indeed, after all the troubles she has overcome and considerable property she acquired, now it is time for her to go.

MOTHER: You're quite right. I'm back where I started. . .

SEOK-CHUL: *(Continues singing.)* Therefore, she made up her mind to have a *kut* for a living death performed, offering up all her worldly treasures in order to go to heaven.

1ST SON: That bum is a mugger without a knife! I already paid one million *won* but he wants all her property. . .[7]

MOTHER: Don't get all bothered, son. He's just chanting the prologue of the *kut* for a living death. That's the way it should be. Please let it go.

SEOK-CHUL: *(Continues reading.)* Therefore, she wishes to have a lavish after-life in paradise and wishes to rejoin her long-lost husband there, enjoying happiness with him. That's why she now knocks on the door to heaven. . . .

GONG PLAYER: *(Chorusing.)* Eol-ssu.[8]

Enter the FEMALE SHAMAN ASSISTANT. *Holding a water-dipping gourd, she sings the first stanza of the shaman song, "Chungbo," which is similar to the "Menari," a popular folk melody in the Kangweon and Kyeongsang districts[9] of Korea.*

FEMALE SHAMAN ASSISTANT: *(Singing cunningly, to invite the spirits.)* [10]

Il Swae Dong Bang Kyeol Do Rang
I Swae Nam Bang Deuk Cheong Rang
Sam Swae Seo Bang Gu Jeong To
Sa Swae Buk Bang Yeong An Gang
Do Rang Cheong Jeong Mu Ha E
Sam Bo Ha E Sam Bo Cheon Ryong Gang Cha Ji
A Geum Ji Song Mo Jin Eon
Weon Sa Ja Bi Mil Ga Ho
A Seok So Jo Je Ak Eop
Gae Yu Mu Si Tam Jin Chi
Jong Sin Gu Ui Ji So Saeng
Il Che A Geum Gae Cham Hwoe
Om Sal Ba Mojja Mojji Sa Da Ya Sa Ba Ha A.

This song is called "Doryanggye," taken from the Cheonsu-kyeong,[11] *which is used to purify the air of the kut performance. The* FEMALE SHAMAN ASSISTANT *sings this song while sprinkling water from her gourd on the audience, though not enough to offend them. Putting down the empty gourd, she lights a candle, and begins to dance.*

FEMALE SHAMAN: *(singing)*
Let's wash out the stains on the altar.
Let's cleanse and rinse away.
Selecting portraits of the ancestors,
Handing them to heroes,
Let's eliminate the stained portraits.
Clean portraits
Wash away the bad portraits . . .
GONG PLAYER: *(Chorusing.)* Eol-ssu!

(As the FEMALE ASSISTANT *fades away, dancing upstage.)*

SEOK-CHUL: That's enough! Let's begin. *(Singing in Chang style.)* E — e —yeo-heun-yeo —yeoheunyeo —yeoheunyeo — *(Sympathetically.)* Heo — i!— What a terribly pity for her whose precious bosom is now wrinkled. Who could know her hard life, and who could know it's time for her to go to the Other World. *(Half crying.)* Now, I'd like to be next to my ancestors, cutting all ties to this world. But, alas, where is the person I can confide it, and which of my children will understand what I have done in my life? Ahh, ack, ack, ah ahck. . . . *(Fully in tears.)*[12]
1ST SON: Is he trying to piss me off?

(MOTHER wipes her eyes with her handkerchief.)

SEOK-CHUL: *(Yelling.)* What have all my troubles been for? Who waits for a good time to get into heaven? *(Pointing at the 1ST SON.)* They say heaven is a paradise, but who doesn't prefer everyday living with their kids. Alas! *(Pointing at the granddaughter among the kut audience.)* She should get married to the son of a great man like Jo Ja-Ryong and produce a son while I'm alive. Alas! It's too late. Don't tell me you're coming in whatever season. Please leave me alone! Don't keep telling me to go anywhere. *(Yelling even louder.)* I won't go, never will go!

MOTHER *bursts into tears. Shaking his head, the* 1ST SON *smokes a cigarette with a grimace. His* WIFE*'s mouth begins to tremble.* MOTHER *cries louder.* SEOK-CHUL *continues crying in a sad mood, watching the reaction of the kut audience, while the* FEMALE SHAMAN ASSISTANT *goes to center stage to help him.*

FEMALE SHAMAN: *(Singing in Chang style.)* I go, I go, I gotta go. To— Yeo— To the Yeol-shee Kingdom,[13] I go— Yeo— If I die today, I would have no chance to see my sons again, and they would search around to find their mom.— Oh— Oh— Oh— Where is my mom? How can I live without her?. . .

At this point, the 1ST SON *turns his face away hysterically, tears brimming in his eyes. Collapsing on his* MOTHER*'s bosom, he cries, "Mother," not wanting to part with his money.*

MOTHER: *(She stops crying abruptly, beating her son on his head)* Money, please! You should pull out some cash right now! *(She starts crying again, her eyes directing him to place some money on the altar. The 1ST SON tearfully looks for his wallet, which is not in his pockets.)* 1ST SON: Mom. . . I don't have any money!

Still crying, the MOTHER *draws some cash out of a tobacco pouch, shaking the bills. Still crying, the 1ST SON snatches them and puts them in the belt of the* FEMALE SHAMAN.

SEOK-CHUL: Supplication! Supplication! Supplication to everybody. Let them go to the Do-ri stream, Let them go to the Round Trip stream—*(SEOK-CHUL is walking around the auditorium with a bamboo container, taking donations from the theatre audience.)* When you give me a donation, it is not for nothing. You give it to me for the necessities of Mrs. Lee Bok-Nye who will journey to heaven. Now, let's give her some money; hey, you gentlemen, let me have five hundred *won*; hey, you good looking ladies, let me have one hundred *won* each; if you donate, you will meet your ideal spouse. Donation, donation, you ladies and gentlemen, donation, donation, all you saintly ladies and gentlemen, donation.

MOTHER: Hey, Seok-Chul, you're going too far. Get back to the *kut* performance, you crazy bum. If you indulge yourself in counting money, the *kut* spirit will leave.

SEOK-CHUL: *(aside)* She is such an old bitch, I can't conjure the spirit anyhow. *(To her.)* You got it, let's continue. Let's move to a new tune for the living.

(Light-heartedly singing in Chang style.)

Those born in the year of Rooster, Snake, and Bull have bad luck for three years. Let's ward off the eight disasters during those three years. Sam-Chung-Sal, Yuk-Chung-Sal, Sam-Jae-Pal-Nan Cheong-Yong-Sal Gam-Ki-Mom-Sal Gae-Pak-Sal Dong-Ki-Gan-E Ae-Jung-Sal Bu-Pu-Gan-E I-Byeol-Sal A-Pa-Tu-E Son-Jae Sal-Gil-Geot-Da-Ga Yun-Hwa-Sal: Keep all these Sals away from me—Oh, I'm out of breath—Let's keep going to the "luck oratorio." *(Continuing in Chang style.)* In-Bok Deul-Go Yeo-Bok Deul-Go Mul-Bok Dul-Go Soe-Bok Deul-Go Gwan-Bok Deul-Myeon O-Bok-I-Yo.

One year, twelve months, three hundred sixty days
Counting July, February to August, and March to September,
Over April to October, May to December, June to November,
Till Spring, Summer, Fall, and Winter are gone,
Comforting family, ever forever,
Producing male and female baby each,
All goes well with industry, agriculture, commerce, and education,
Enough to eat, enough to use, enough to wear,
Everyone enjoys days and nights in a wonderful life.
(To the MOTHER.*)* I'm done, folks, I'm finished. It's over. *(He looks very tired.)*

MOTHER: You aren't good as you use to be. *(Clucking her tongue.)* You ran out power because you slept around too much when you were young.

SEOK-CHUL: What the hell are you talking about? I didn't sleep around, but I got ripped off by betting on *mah-jong* when I was young.

These days, I lose all my money to pachinko. *(Shaking his head agitatedly.)* Put me in the old folks group from now on.

MOTHER: Don't make me laugh! Get back to performing "O-Gu the Great."

SEOK-CHUL: *(Stunned, as though he had been struck.)* You do it by yourself, Grandma! *(Grunting.)* How can I perform when I'm all out of breath?

1ST SON: *(As he gets a chance to interrupt.)* What the hell is this? Stop performing!? You're trying to rip off my one million *won* with this charade, aren't you? That's enough! Knock it off! I'm not gonna pay the other half.

SEOK-CHUL: *(Repulsed.)* What the hell is this treatment? Hey, look, who said it's one million *won*? This is the forth performance for the living death of your mother. The first one cost one million *won* six years ago. Now it costs more than that; you know, there is such a thing as inflation.

1ST SON: What are you talking about? The *kut* doesn't cost anything to perform. Inflation is not an issue here, you grafter!

SEOK-CHUL: You watch your mouth! I've been performing this for more than fifty years, ever since I was a seven year-old boy. I learned this with sweat and blood. These days some sham performers without any training make their money doing pseudo-performances. Compared to them, I am a professional.

MOTHER: You rotten louts! Is this *kut* a place for you to fight? *(Tossing her money pouch to* SEOK-CHUL.*)* Here we go, the money! That's all I got. I don't need any money any more! Would you please put your heart into the performance of "O-Gu the Great"?

SEOK-CHUL: *(Aside.)* I can't take her pouch money because it stinks like hell. *(To the* 1ST SON.*)* Don't worry. It's not over yet, so would you take a seat over there, and just enjoy the performance, please? This is how it should be, you know, like in the script's stage direction. How come you misunderstand that? *(To the* MOTHER.*)* Grandma, since I'm all out of stamina to perform the *kut* by myself these days, *(Pointing at the* FEMALE ASSISTANT.*)* I've paid for the hired assistant. She's good. Gently to hear, please.

MOTHER: She can't keep a beat; she's so young.

SEOK-CHUL: No, no. It's all right. The younger, the better, these days. *(Playing the Janggo, a double-headed, hour-glass-shaped drum.)* Now, *(Singing in Chang style.)* It's a *kut* performance, it's a *kut* performance . . . .

FEMALE SHAMAN: *(Follows him, singing in Chang style, too.)* It's a *kut* performance, it's a *kut* performance. This kut performance is for who. . .

SEOK-CHUL: Eo— Eu-ya.

FEMALE SHAMAN: Is this *kut* for the Sun? Or is this *kut* for the Moon? Hi — Eo —Ya.

SEOK-CHUL: Eo— Eu— Eya.

FEMALE SHAMAN: It's for fun, just for fun, everything is for fun. One hundred years fly, indeed, like a dream.

SEOK-CHUL and MOTHER: Eo— Euya.

FEMALE SHAMAN: As a ghost when I die, coming back to my home town, Born with bare body and hands, trying to live a hundred years, What have I done since I was born into this world?

It's so sad, so sad, everything is so sad for mankind.

SEOK-CHUL and MOTHER: *(Half crying.)* Eo— Eu— Eya.

FEMALE SHAMAN: *(Getting faster, little by little.)*

They say the other world's far from here, where I am heading.

When we die, we've gone forever.

Everyone's too busy living to notice anything ahead.

MOTHER: Well done!

FEMALE SHAMAN: Farewell, farewell, Smoothing the way with prayer to Amida Buddha,[14] Taking the decomposed hand of my dead husband without shunning,

Long live the reunited couple without complaining of the Other World.

MOTHER: All right, I'll do it.

The MOTHER *stands and starts dancing.* SEOK-CHUL*'s drum playing increases in intensity.*

MOTHER: There's no disease in the Other World. And no senility, either. I'll travel around Paradise, re-united with my husband, hand in hand.

SEOK-CHUL and MOTHER: Eol-Ssu!

FEMALE SHAMAN: *(In a quick tempo.)* Bless their reunited souls,

Their love will start a blaze,

Their sight will never dim,

Their backs will never stoop,

Their hearing will never fade,

Their behavior will be decent forever.

SEOK-CHUL and MOTHER: Eol-Ssu! That's good!

FEMALE SHAMAN: Skip along on your legs with full vigor, please.

(Singing.) Let's enjoy, let's enjoy, while we're young.

As we grow older, to enjoy nothing is our loss.

All that's fair must fade and the full moon soon wanes.

(All, chorusing.) Eol-Ssi-Gu, Jeol-Ssi-Gu, Cha-Cha-Cha,

Ji-Hwa-Ja, Jo-Ku-Nah, Cha-Cha-Cha.
Life is but a walking shadow,
So carpe diem, and seize the day, eol-ssi-gu!

As SEOK-CHUL *plays his drums "doong, doong, doong, doong, du doong, doong, doong," the* FEMALE SHAMAN ASSISTANT *brings her performance to an end. At that very moment, the* MOTHER, *with a radiant face, calls her* 1ST SON *in a loud voice.*

MOTHER: Tack-Ah, *(Anxiously.)* Tack-Ahaaaaa!
1ST SON: Don't call me 'Tack-Ah', Tack-Ah' here in front of a lot of people, please!

The stage audience bursts out laughing.

MOTHER: *(Her face glowing, but anxious.)* It's time for me to go.

MOTHER *falls senseless to the floor. Everyone is silent.* SEOK-CHUL, *standing up, approaches her.*

SEOK-CHUL *(Stunned.)* She's dead. Grandma Bok-Nye's gone.

All are stock-still, motionless.

SEOK-CHUL: *(Grinning.)* She's gone to heaven.
1ST SON: *(Like a little kid.)* Mommy!

1ST SON *runs to hug her and cry.* SEOK-CHUL *starts singing and playing a drum; a ceremony for her soul begins.*

SEOK-CHUL: I go, I go / Go to Heaven / With prayers to Amida Buddha, now, I go.
The moon/though she's not bright/she's enough to shine/heaven to earth
But it's pitch-black/I don't see/the route to heaven, rough with thorns.
O Gu the Great/please light/the way for me.
Hey, kid/Taking the beat from my drum/Open the route for Grandma,
If time flies/all by itself/Why does it take our parents with it?
During their lives/our parents/Have lived/with troubles,
The journey/to the Other World/is it more comfortable than this world?
Hey, listen/I've a question to ask/All's well in the Other World?

(Starts wailing.)

You, spirit— Ah— spirit, spirit— Ah— spirit
Ringing in my ears/glimmering in my eyes/From where/is it calling me?
Is heaven calling me/or is hell calling me?
Is the air calling me?/The way of the world is like a lotus lantern.
My spirit has come to this world/my soul has come here
But my house/is empty/Uh— Uh— Mountains and streams
Are as before./Green fields and fresh waters
I used to have./My kids on my back in this house/I used to reside/
Shell of my body/100 year shell of my body,
Where are you? Are you leaving me just like that?
Uh-Hwa-Neom-Cha Daengurang Daeng Daeng tears in my eyes ,
Can't see the way to the Bukmang Mountain.
Ah— Uhuh— Neo gari Numcha Neo Neo Neo Uh gari Numcha
NeoNeo Uh—Neogari neomcha neoheo Daengrang Daeng Daeng
(Fade lights.) Nuhgari Numcha Nuhnuhho Uhnuhho Uhgari
Numchaho Uhhuh Nugari Numcha Nuhnuhnuh Uhgari Numcha
Nuhnuh . . . .

(Black out in silence. Then. . .)

Ah— Ee— Goh— *(Scene changes with chorusing in low voice.)*

ACT II

A Ceremony for the Dead, Part I—Taking a Body

SEOK-CHUL: In the ritual manual, there are instructions of how to prepare at the moment of death, how to invoke the spirit, how to take care
of the body, how to treat the process during the rite, how to prepare
the coffin, how to send out an obituary, etc. The instructions are as follows: At the moment of death, confirm the last breath. This process,
which I checked for myself previously, should be repeated once again
for audience. *(To the 1ST SON.)* Do it, now! *(The 1ST SON goes to the
prop shelves and tries to find something.)*
SEOK-CHUL: Grab the feather, the feather!
1ST SON: I know, but where the hell is it? Ah, here we go!
MOTHER: *(Places the feather under the MOTHER's nose.)* Stop tickling me.
1ST SON: Isn't this the way it's supposed to be done?
SEOK-CHUL: What the hell are you doing now? Knock it off and get
on with it.

MOTHER: You're tickling me!

SEOK-CHUL: A dead body is not supposed to feel anything! *(To the* MOTHER.*)* Lie down, now. *(To the* 1ST SON.*)* Stop tickling like that; just put it on her nose!

MOTHER: See? You're doing it wrong. Don't tickle me!

The MOTHER *lies down quickly. The* 1ST SON *puts the feather on her nose; the feather flutters.*

SEOK-CHUL: See. The feather is fluttering. That means that she's still breathing. Now, the 1ST son who has confirmed her death removes her jacket. *(The* 1ST SON *takes her jacket off.)* That jacket now changes from a jacket to an apron. Are you waiting for an engraved invitation? Do it, now!

1ST SON: I'm doing it!

The 1ST SON *puts the jacket on his waist as an apron.*

SEOK-CHUL: The next step is "calling the spirit." *(To the* 1ST SON.*)* To the roof!

The 1ST SON *rushes to center stage and steps up the stairs.*

SEOK-CHUL: Call your Mom while you wave that apron.

1ST SON: Mommy . . . . Mommy . . . . Momma . . . .

SEOK-CHUL: What's her name?

1ST SON: Lee Bok-Nye.

SEOK-CHUL: Right, call your mother's name.

1ST SON: Lee Bok-Nye . . . . Lee Bok-Nye . . . . Lee Bok-Nye . . . .

The 1ST SON *steps down from the stairs.*

SEOK-CHUL: Back to your seat! When you step down, use the other side.

1ST SON: The other side.

SEOK-CHUL *approaches the* MOTHER *and holds her legs. The* 1ST SON *holds her shoulders. They lift her up.*

SEOK-CHUL: *(To an actor sitting at the edge of the stage.)* Quit day-dreaming and do something! Go make sure the board is facing south.

Two male actors trim the board southward. They put the MOTHER's *body there, on the board.*

SEOK-CHUL: Bring me the *yut* sticks. *(An ACTRESS brings them, and inserts them into the mouth of the dead body.)* [15]
Then, close the eyes of the deceased.
Tie the feet to the wood frame so they won't twist.
Put the hands on the stomach, and tie the thumbs together.
And tie the big toes together with the other end.
(To ACTRESSES.*)* What are you waiting for? Set the meals for the dead in the yard now. Don't forget that offerings for the dead are comprised of rice, coins, and straw shoes.

ACTRESSES: Why?

SEOK-CHUL: Because there will be three hell-messengers. Now let's begin to make up the body. Stay away, you ladies.

ACTRESSES: Whatever you say.

SEOK-CHUL: First of all, bathing!

MOTHER: First cover me with that sheet then undress me.

SEOK-CHUL: Cover the corpse with that large sheet . . . Wash its face, head, and hands with water of mugwort, with rice-rinsing water, and sweet smelling water. And then . . .wash its feet. Cut its hair, and trim its fingernails and toenails . . .

MOTHER: Skip cutting the hair. *(ACTRESSES mime trimming the MOTHER's nails.)*

SEOK-CHUL: On a mattress covered with a single sheet, insert the upper parts of the garment for the dead between the body and the sheet, then the lower parts of the garment for the dead in the same way. Then dress the corpse with them. Put traditional socks on its feet, a pair of mittens on its hands, a headpiece on its head. Feeding it like this: *(Opens the MOTHER's mouth, and throws a grain of rice into it.)* It's one thousand silos, two thousand silos, three thousand silos of rice. *(While placing a copper coin in her mouth.)* It's one thousand coins, two thousand coins, three thousand coins. Wrap the body twenty-one times.

MOTHER: Easy, easy. This is acting!

SEOK-CHUL: The next step is a Dae-ryum, in other words, en-coffin!

ACTORS 1 *and* 2 *lift the corpse and toss it into the coffin.*

MOTHER: Ow! How dare you throw a dead person around like that!

ACTOR 1 & 2: *(Speaking to each other.)* Easy, easy. This isn't a real funeral.

SEOK-CHUL: Skip tying up the coffin up because it should be open easily later in the ritual.

ACTOR 2: Is this a rehearsal for "Legend's Hometown"?[16]

SEOK-CHUL: Why are we dressing up the dead in such a complicated manner?

ACTOR 1: To play the coquette for Yama.

ACTOR 2: Because we're bored, with little to do.

SEOK-CHUL: You can say that again!

The ACTORS *one by one lay their garments for the Ceremony of the Dead on a thin straw mat in the center of the stage and stand face to face.*[17]

SEOK-CHUL: Everybody, bow!

ALL ACTORS: *(In a low voice.)* Ah— Ee— Goh—

SEOK-CHUL: Put them on, now! Get dressed quickly!

ALL ACTORS: *(Quickening.)* Ah-Ee-Goh Ah-Ee-Goh.

SEOK-CHUL: Now, when you're done, step forward, one by one. *(To* ACTOR 1.*)* You, first . . . *(The* 2ND SON, *played by* ACTOR 1, *steps forward, and strikes a pose like a fashion model.)*
The authentic way to wear them is too difficult to follow. Authenticity is good for classic plays, but these days, we don't need to follow authentic practices. *(To the* 2ND SON.*)* If you're not married, don't put on the headpiece. Bind your head with hemp rope; put your arm in only one sleeve. *(Touching his shoulder.)* Expose your shoulder like this, as if you're an idiot. And leave your garment open. Loosen it! *(The* WIFE *of the* 1ST SON *steps forward and strikes a pose like a model.)* The wife of the chief mourner should let down her hair and wear a cheap garment made of cotton cloth. You wear this cheap cloth to show your penitence during the funeral ceremony. Now, get inside the house and show your penitence. *(*ACTRESS 1 *steps forward quickly.)* The ladies who are not related to the chief mourner should affix this wooden hairpin in a northerly to the head of the corpse. *(To the* 1ST SON.*)* Are you ready?

1ST SON: Just a second. *(He appears in a fully decorated mourner's garment.)*

SEOK-CHUL: The first son mourner should wear a mourning garment in full decoration, because he represents all the family members. *(Pointing at the garment.)* It's composed of the hemp hat, a hemp hair band, hemp coat, hemp sashes, pants, leggings, stockings and straw sandals.

ACTOR 1: I have to play one of the sons from Act III on; how come my garment looks so shabby?

SEOK-CHUL: The sons are all different. Mourning house rules say "first come, first served." Now, everybody is ready, let's begin.

Scene change followed by a song, then. . .

SEOK-CHUL: Hey, since you're taking the role of the second son, you shouldn't count the obituary money. *(Pointing to* ACTOR 2.*)* You take care of it. *(To the* WIFE *of the* 1ST SON.*)* What are you eating now? Didn't I tell you you should show your penitence . . . Keep starving during the funeral ceremony.

1ST SON'S WIFE: What the hell! Can't mourners have any food during the ceremony?

SEOK-CHUL: Only soup is allowed, but not now, later. No food for the mourners, but thin soup is allowed.

1ST SON'S WIFE: I didn't have lunch.

SEOK-CHUL: Well, then, go and get something to eat back stage, right now. *(To the* 1ST SON, *who is smoking.)* Put it out. *(To the lighting booth.)* Take out the lights. *(Blackout on the entire stage. The cigarette flame is flickering.)*

ACT III

A Ceremony for the Dead, Part II—A House in Mourning

SEOK-CHUL: *(Mourning halfheartedly.)* Aigo, Aigo, Aigo.

FEMALE CONDOLER 1: The other day, when I attended another house in mourning, I had a real laugh at the-daughter-in-law's way of mourning. She mourned "ho— ho—" like a goat.

FEMALE CONDOLER 2: Sounding like a goat crying isn't the only thing to laugh at, you know.

FEMALE CONDOLER 1: Well, as a matter of fact, all things in a house of mourning are laughable.

SEOK-CHUL: A-aigo, aigo, aigo, get me something to eat, quick, won't you? Aigo, I'm starving to death after mourning so many hours straight. Oh boy, my stomach keeps growling, and my navel touches my back. Get me something, P-L-E-A-S-E—

1ST SON'S WIFE: It's on its way.

1ST SON: Mourning for hours without a break is really hard, you know.

1ST SON'S WIFE: If it's hard, how come you put him up to it? You're the one who is supposed to do it by himself, aren't you?

SEOK-CHUL: Aigo, I'm starving.

The 1ST SON'S WIFE *rudely places a low meal table in front of him.*

SEOK-CHUL What the hell. . . . Why are you throwing dog food at me?

1ST SON'S WIFE: There must be a hundred beggars in your stomach.

SEOK-CHUL: How do you think I keep mourning on an empty stomach?

1ST SON'S WIFE: Who's going to eat cheerfully in the house of mourning? Please behave yourself in this house. You get paid for mourning!

SEOK-CHUL: What the hell are you talking about? As a special invitee, it's my job to break the mournful air of the house! *(The* 1ST SON'S WIFE *retires peevishly.)*

SEOK-CHUL: *(Chewing a mouthful of rice.)* Aigo —

Enter MALE CONDOLER 1.

SEOL CHUL: A condoler is coming, aigo—

The 1ST SON *stands up abruptly, adjusting his garment.* MALE CONDOLER 2, *after placing money in a condolence envelope on a low table, faces the funerary table and kneels down on the straw mat. He lights incense, then bows deeply two and a half times.*

1ST SON: Aigo.

CONDOLERS: Hui.

1ST SON: Aigo, aigo—

CONDOLER 1: Hui, hui.

CONDOLER 2: This must be a burden for you. . .

1ST SON: I appreciate your coming when you are so busy. . .

CONDOLER 1: It's good she lived out her natural life.

1ST SON: What am I supposed to reply to that?

CONDOLER 1: Just say "Thank you."

1ST SON: Thank you.

SEOK-CHUL: Cut the crap, stop kowtowing, and come over here. Let's prepare the spirit food offering. Madam, would you do the invocation, please?

1ST SON: Honey— Seok-Chul said it's your turn to prepare food offering for the spirit. . .

1ST SON'S WIFE: I don't know how to do it.

SEOK-CHUL: I taught you just a little while ago, didn't I?

1ST SON'S WIFE: Isn't it enough for me just to wail?

SEOK-CHUL: To just wail?

1ST SON'S WIFE: Do I have to follow the traditional way?

SEOK-CHUL: Not only that, you have to act, too.

1ST SON'S WIFE: I don't buy it. I'm going to cry out naturally

SEOK-CHUL: No, you should not. If you do it naturally, you'll lose your voice and harm your throat. Just do it the way I teach you. That is the easiest way for both the dead and the living. Watch me. Bring this meal table to the funerary table, offering a cup of rice wine, then make a big bow, touching your cheek with the skirt held in your hand, and cry, aigo, aigo, like this. At that moment, you, the father of Bong-Suk, begin crying aego, aego, aego. . . Got it? Loosen up your throat, inhale enough air to expand the belly and exhale smoothly. Do not try to cry out naturally, okay?

1ST SON: Gotcha!

SEOK-CHUL: *(To* CONDOLER 1.*)* Now, it's our turn. Let's bow to each other.

CONDOLER 1: Right.

SEOK-CHUL: *(Kneeling down and making a great bow to him.)* I am a professional here to mourn as the chief mourner.

CONDOLER 1: *(Instantly bowing, with a smile on his face.)* I am the eldest grandson in the head-family of Lee at Yoeju and one of the relatives of the dead, *(Handing* SEOK-CHUL *his name card.).* . . Here we go; I am a man of no special significance.

SEOK-CHUL: *(Taking the name card and reading it.)* General director of the Union for Liberty, Jongno district branch office; Executive Committee Member and Director of Relationships in the Buddhist Organization for the Defense of Korea, Jongno branch. . . uh, I didn't recognize that you're a man of high position.[18]

CONDOLER 1: I'm a real estate broker with an office just cross the street.

SEOK-CHUL: I see. It's good for us to meet new faces and say "hello" to each other.

CONDOLER 1: Of course. That's the way we should live, isn't it?

SEOK-CHUL: Let's play cards.

WIDOW: *(To* SEOK-CHUL.*)* How are you doing, sir?

SEOK-CHUL: Oh, geez, I'm sorry. You are. . .?

WIDOW: I am Bong-Suk's aunt on her mother's side, don't you remember me? I was here to participate in the *kut* last year.

SEOK-CHUL: Oh, it's you. I am so sorry not to recognize you.

WIDOW: Is the spirit food offering under way?

SEOK-CHUL: Please lend a hand. Since the second son is still single, the eldest son's wife is having a hard time doing it all by herself.

WIDOW, *who takes off her shoes quietly, bursts out in mourning, sitting on the straw mat. The* WIDOW*'s mourning gets attention from those in* *attendance on stage, since it is so loud and flowing. Accordingly, the 1ST and 2ND SONS genuinely cry, sobbing much, and then the 1ST SON'S WIFE begins mourning. At that moment, CONDOLERS 1 and 3 enter. The face of the granddaughter, BON-SUK, peeps in.*

GRANDDAUGHTER: Grandma. Heuk, heuk. *(Sobbing.)*
SEOK-CHUL: Hey, Bong-Suk! Bring me a bottle of *soju* and a dish of sliced pig head meat, will you!
GRANDDAUGHTER: Ahk. *(Retreats sulkily.)*

Black out, the 1ST SON, the 2ND SON, and the 1ST SON'S WIFE crying increasingly. Lights up.

SEOK-CHUL: Shuffle 'em.
CONDOLER 1: Ante up, please.
SEOK-CHUL: Money is easy come, easy go. *(To CONDOLER 2.)* Lend me ten thousand *won*, will you?
CONDOLER 2: Give me one reason why I should lend you some cash.
SEOK-CHUL: It's not right for us to not to lend some cash when playing cards.
CONDOLER 3: Why don't you lend him ten thousand *won* now, and get it back with big interest later?
CONDOLER 1: If you're out of cash, get back to the funerary table and start mourning. You said you're a professional.
SEOK-CHUL: Don't tell me what to do, you crazy bum.
CONDOLER 1: What did you say? Crazy bum? Are you out of your mind? You look down on me because I'm a broker?
SEOK-CHUL: No, I'm not looking down on you— I'm ignoring you!
CONDOLER 1: What? Ignoring me?
CONDOLER 2: Stop fighting about nothing, like kids, *(To SEOK-CHUL.)* and get some cash, okay? You're old enough to know the rules, aren't you?
CONDOLER 3: Let's get back to the game without him.
SEOK-CHUL: *(Approaches the 1ST SON.)* Would you pay me in advance, please?
1ST SON: All out of cash?
SEOK-CHUL: I wailed my best today for nothing because I'm already completely broke.
1ST SON: You don't know how to play cards. *(1ST SON approaches the players.)*
SEOK-CHUL: Shuffle' em.

CONDOLER 2: *(To the* 1ST SON, *ignoring* SEOK-CHUL.*)* Are you in?

SEOK-CHUL: I'm out for a while, because I'm a little tired.

CONDOLER 2: One thousand per point, "Radiant" cards are better. It's Chun Du-Whan Go-Stop game, okay? [19] *(Cards are dealt.)*

1ST SON: Five matching cards rule or six?

CONDOLER 1: It's six matching cards rule, the "Radiant" cards are one thousand won, minimum card rule and calling "go" three times means double points.

Game commences, with players quickly selecting and discarding cards with sharply punctuated motions.

1ST SON: Go!

CONDOLER 3: Go! What the hell! *(CONDOLER 3 gives up the game.)*

CONDOLER 2: How come? Giving up, again?

CONDOLER 3: Why not? I won't keep playing with bad cards.

CONDOLER 2: Are you playing for "Radiant" cards only? Shame on you. Don't give him cards next hand. *(Game continues energetically.)*

CONDOLER 3: You shouldn't be talking big with small change in your pocket.

CONDOLER 2: I don't need to talk big to you. I don't need your vote!

CONDOLER 3: Vote? You?

1ST SON: *(Having matched the right number of cards, he elects not to end this hand, but to take a chance to increase his winnings by calling "go" which means another round of cards being played.)* Well, I got three points, but call "go." I got lucky early, which is great!

CONDOLER 3: Early luck will drive you into bankruptcy at last.

The WIDOW *brings a new serving table with another bottle of wine, twitching her fanny very coquettishly. The card players stare at her, stunned. Soon, she retires into the kitchen, wagging her tail voluptuously.*

SEOK-CHUL: *(To* CONDOLER 1.*)* Pay attention! *(Begins the "Muak," a shaman dance using the gong and drum.)*

SEOK-CHUL: *(To the* WIDOW.*)* Is your throat open wide?

WIDOW: Will you squeeze me in if I sing a tune?

SEOK-CHUL: Well, of course. Huh, huh hut. *(Laughing suggestively.)*

WIDOW: Ohoooo.

1ST SON'S WIFE: Somebody, give me a bowl of gruel.

SEOK-CHUL: Is it hard for you to be the chief mourner's wife?

WIFE: Not really, but I'm starved to death.

SEOK-CHUL: From now on, you'll be very tired because you can't sleep for next three days

The 2ND SON, shouting, "Give me a bowl of gruel, please!" takes a seat in the card game.

1ST SON: Well, I got three points, and call, "go" three times.

CONDOLER 3: The chief mourner is on his luck today.

1ST SON: Well, it's nothing to talk about.

CONDOLER 2: Wait a minute. . . *(Picking up a card from beneath the straw mat.)* What is this? Why, you double-dealer! *(Every player stares at the 1ST SON.)*

1ST SON: No, I'm not.

CONDOLER 2: *(Grabbing his collar.)* You low-life! Cough 'em up. Cough 'em all, you son-of-a-bitch.

1ST SON: What? You rootless bastards!

CONDOLER 3: This game is over, done, finished! *(Quickly gathering up the money.)*

1ST SON: *(Shaking off their arms.)* Let me go, you rootless hypocrites!

(In the master bedroom.)

2ND SON: What's the matter with him? *(Referring to the 1ST SON.)*

1ST SON'S WIFE: He has a weakness for cards . . .

2ND SON: Great, what a pretty kettle of fish! I will get out of this house this time.

1ST SON'S WIFE: Go on! Who's stopping you?

SEOK-CHUL: *(In Chang tune.)* Uh—huh—eu Namseonbujung, Republic of Korea, Seoul city, Jongno ward, Hyewha district, Lee's mourning house. Please go to Heaven shaking off all the troubles of this world, burning all the sins you committed in this world. Let's bathe in the Dongnae hot springs. She is taking her steps in the wide fields of Beobseong.

(At the playing cards mat.)

CONDOLER 1: *(Playing cards.)* What a wonderful song!

CONDOLER 2: Would you sing a little louder, please? Let the living and the dead enjoy the song together.

SEOK-CHUL: As the sinful hands are floating the day-to-day loan, when Gwang Mok Cheon-Wang makes his appearance,[20] why don't you try to learn Cheongbojang from me.

WIDOW: Okay!

(In the master bedroom.)

2ND SON: Let's sell this house if brother says okay. These days, apartments are a hot investment, you know?

1ST SON'S WIFE: Can we buy two apartments by selling this house?

2ND SON: This a big house, worth about 300,000,000 *won.*[21]

1ST SON'S WIFE: And then?

2ND SON: I'm not saying that I will launch the business with the money by myself. You can audit the books.

1ST SON'S WIFE: Forget about audits and board of directors. I don't want to hear about audits and boards of directors. Don't you remember you squandered our fortune lately? Have you no shame?

SEOK-CHUL: *(His tune increases in intensity).* Sangji is rising? Or the moon is rising?

Ah, uh— U-Ryang-Jeon-Ha Dae-Beob-Chang-A. How do I do? Eeh— *(Muak continues.* SEOK-CHUL *and the* WIDOW *start shoulder-dancing.)*[22]

Buk-Eun-Cheon-Wang Hu-Bang-Cheon-Wang-A U-Ri-Jung Jung-Wang U-Ma-Dang-A Sam-Sip-Sam-Cheon-E I-Sip-Pal-Su-Ya

SEOK-CHUL and WIDOW: Yuk-Jang-Mun-A Gu-Cheong-Gu-Wo I Eo-Seu-Ya

Nu-Un Cheon-Ja Ok-Jang-Mun Yeol-Go Na-Mu-Geum-Su Ha-Dan-Mun Yeol-Go Eo—Hu—

CARD PLAYERS: Bravo, Eol-Ssa— *(Card players begin shoulder-dancing while playing cards.)*

SEOK-CHUL and WIDOW: Jung-Ang-Whang-Yu-Ri Wha-Jang-Se-Gae Sang-Ju-Seol-Beob Ha-Op-Si-Go.

CARD PLAYERS: *(To* SEOK-CHUL *and* WIDOW.*)* That's great!

Suddenly, SEOK-CHUL *rings the bell.*

SEOK-CHUL: Guests are coming—

1ST SON: *(Reluctantly puts cards down and dons the headpiece.)* Who the hell is coming to mourn this late at night . . .

(Enter the MESSENGERS *from the Other World.)*

WIDOW: Kwacccck!

Black out.

ACT IV

A Ceremony for the Dead, Part III—Messengers from the Other World

When the lights come up again, the scene goes back to the last moment of Act III when the WIDOW *sees one of the* MESSENGERS *from the Other World. All are frozen in place.*

SEOK-CHUL: *(Standing up calmly.)* Welcome! You arrived early today.

MESSENGER 1: Long time no see. *(Shaking hands.)* Take care of yourself, Seok-Chul. Your name is on the list lately. *(Referring to the* WIDOW.*)* This lady shocked me. I almost passed out.

SEOK-CHUL: *(Pointing at the* 1ST SON.*)* That guy over there is the chief mourner today.

MESSENGER 1: *(To the* 1ST SON.*)* Well, how do you do?

1ST SON: *(Taking off the headpiece in a moment of bewilderment, and bowing.)* My name is Sang Taek-Choe. I've heard your name before, but to meet you in person—

MESSENGER 1: —is the first time. If you meet us messengers from the Other World a second time that means . . . you know what I mean?

SEOK-CHUL: Well, shall we go inside? I guess you folks are starving now, since you have traveled such a long way. *(Pointing at the sumptuous feast table for the dead.)* This way, please. . .

MESSENGERS: *(To those in the house.)* Well, we'll take our seats at the table if you insist.

MESSENGER 1 *enters the house, shaking hands while bowing to the* 1ST SON, 2ND SON, CONDOLER 1, CONDOLER 2, *and* CONDOLER 3, *respectively. It is obvious in the faces of* MESSENGERS 2 *and* 3 *that they are apprehensive as well as curious. As they take seats at the table, the* WIDOW *quickly brings a kettle of rice wine and a dish of sliced pig-head meat.*

MESSENGER 1: Oh, no, please. According to regulations, I can't have meat or wine. . .

MESSENGER 2: *(Receiving a meal table.)* Thank you very much. *(To* MESSENGER 1.*)* Look, let's turn a blind eye and eat what's offered this time. Rules take second place to hunger.

MESSENGER 1: You got an official reprimand last month for eating in violation of regulations and you still can't take care of business and abstain! You violate the rules once more, you'll be on your way to Red China. Understand? [23]

MESSENGER 2: They'll send me on my way to Red China or to Gwangju of 1980 for violating regulations?[24] We have to be there, on the emergency alert, when hundreds of dead bodies are coming in. *(To MESSENGER 3.)* Hey, you've been to Red China, haven't you?

MESSENGER 3: *(Sullenly.)* Yes, I have.

MESSENGER 2: Did you get some bribe from Deng Xiaoping? [25]

MESSENGER 3: Not at all. One messenger carried him a hundred dead bodies like a bunch of fish, but the messenger got not so much as a dim-sum.

MESSENGER 1: That's because China is a most uncivilized country.

MESSENGER 2: But it was a paradise compared to Gwangju of 1980; I got bronchitis from the tear gas. *(To MESSENGER 1.)* Did you get rid of that Hong Kong syphilis?

MESSENGER 1: Almost.

MESSENGER 2: You can't say it's completely cured, if you say, "almost".

MESSENGER 1: I know. That's why I am not going to chase skirts any more or have anything to do with women. Beware of women!

MESSENGER 2: This isn't Hong Kong, you know. *(While peeping at the* WIDOW.*)* She's some bomb-foxy, juicy chick. . .

MESSENGER 1: Shut up. A hefty payment would be good.

While MESSENGERS *are talking, the living discuss remuneration for the* MESSENGERS.

SEOK-CHUL: Are you ready?

1ST SON: How much money do I need?

SEOK-CHUL: According to tradition, all you get from the condolence money.

1ST SON'S WIFE: That makes no sense. How come they need cash for the Other World?

SEOK-CHUL: Are we in the Other World, now? They are here, in our world.

1ST SON: True. Let me see, *(Checking the condolence receipts log.)* What is this? It's a blank page! Where is the money? *(Looks in a condolence envelope.)* Oh, shit! There is no cash. It's empty!

CONDOLER 1: What are you talking about?

CONDOLER 2: I paid one hundred thousand *won*!

CONDOLER 3: *(Raising his hand.)* It's me who didn't pay the money.

1ST SON: There already are more than a hundred condolers here. . . .Hey, Kim, Kim!

KIM: Coming. . .

1ST SON: What's going on here?

KIM: What are you talking about?

1ST SON: Are you sure that every single condolence amount is recorded in this book, and the money put down here . . . .

KIM: *(Pointing at the* 2ND *SON.)* Ask him, please.

2ND SON: What's all the fuss about? I took care of the cash, here in my pocket.

1ST SON: Who gave you permission to do that?

2ND SON: You know, this a world where we have to look out for ourselves. Haven't you heard that mourning houses are frequently robbed? *(Taking an envelope from his pocket.)* Here we go, give it to the messengers.

SEOK-CHUL: This is not enough . . . .

2ND SON: Well, then, take some notes from the funeral table and that will do it. *(Grabs some notes from the funeral table, gives them to SEOK-CHUL.)* There you are.

SEOK-CHUL: *(Handing them to KIM.)* Give 'em these.

KIM: Not a chance! I'm scared of them.

2ND SON: You're scared? They are not human beings; they're messengers from the Other World.

KIM: Didn't you see them slap me on the cheek just a while ago?

2ND SON: All right. I'll do it. *(The* 2ND SON *approaches* MESSENGER 2 *hesitantly.)*

Thank you for coming this late at night.

MESSENGER 2: I'm so sorry. Your loss must be a great burden.

2ND SON: Please take this for your traveling expenses. Sorry, it may not be enough.

MESSENGER 2: *(Taking it with feigned reluctance.)*. Ah, you shouldn't have. . .

2ND SON: Would you excuse me . . . .

MESSENGER 2: Of course. *(Peeping into the envelope as soon as the* 2ND SON *turns his back.)* What is this? Is he trying to make me mad? I hate humans. I really do. Oh, how the world is changed, indeed. *(To MESSENGER 1.)* Hey, look. *(Referring to the money.)* Is this the way for humans to treat us these days?

MESSENGER 1: That's pretty disappointing!

MESSENGER 2: We have to do something. Let's make the body jump up from the coffin and dance awake.

MESSENGER 1: Hey, don't do it. We are the messengers from the Other World. We have to behave ourselves. *(Handing a blank check to MES-SENGER 3.)* Here, exchange this blank check for cash.

MESSENGER 3: Where is the bank?

MESSENGER 1: *(Pointing to the* 2ND *SON.)* The gut of that guy is the bank. *(They count the money from the* 2ND *SON and talk.)*

1ST SON: *(To the* 2ND *SON.)* Hey, Number 2, come here a sec. *(The* 2ND *SON approaches the* 1ST *SON.)* Cough it up.

2ND SON: I can't do that.

1ST SON: What! You're such a thief!

2ND SON: You're calling me a thief?

1ST SON: Do you think I am an idiot? I know you took Mother's sealing stamp and bank book already.

2ND SON: Yes, I did. Why not? Anyway, where is the title to the house?

1ST SON: Right here. Title registration, house register, and the certificate of title to this house, I took them all. Any problems?

2ND SON: That's so sticky-fingered! How come you took the papers to Mom's house?

1ST SON: *(Pointing at a contract.)* Who signed this? The dead mother rose from her coffin and signed this sales contract with Happiness Real Estate Inc., did she? Hmmmm?

MESSENGER 3 can't interrupt and stands hesitantly beside the quarreling brothers.

1ST SON: *(Pointing at* CONDOLER 1.) You're in cahoots with this guy to sell the house right out from under me!

2ND SON: Damn it! Use your thick head! How we could we manage the huge inheritance tax? I did my best to write a phony contract two days before she died. . . .

1ST SON: You son-of-a-bitch. *(Butting* 2ND *SON's nose with his head.)*

2ND SON: My nose!

1ST SON: *(Grabbing the* 2ND *SON by the collar.)* Speak up! Who did this piece of work?

2ND SON: I didn't do it by myself! Sister-in-law gave me permission.

1ST SON: *(Pause.)* What the hell . . . *(Standing up abruptly.)* Let's die all together . . . *(*1ST *SON dashes to his* WIFE *and they fall down together as he clings to her waist.)*

1ST SON'S WIFE: Help me!

When she screams, all the characters on the stage, except for the MES-SENGERS and the 2ND *SON, create a panoramic scene of utter confu-*

sion in slow-motion. At that moment, MESSENGER 3 *writes "one hun-dred thousand won" on the check with a pen and puts it front in nose of the* 2ND SON.

2ND SON: What's this?

MESSENGER 3: This check for 100,000 *won*? Messenger 1 asked me to get cash for this.

2ND SON: Do I look like a bank?

SEOK-CHUL: Just cash it. If you irritate him, the funeral ceremony will turn topsy-turvy.

2ND SON: You're a bare-faced crook.

MESSENGER 1: *(Disingenuously.)* What's going on over there?

MESSENGER 2: The human world is a mess. *(Looking at* MESSEN-GER 3 *who is crawling.)* What's the matter with you?

MESSENGER 3: The messenger's back is broken by mankind's fight-ing. Here we go, cash for the check.

MESSENGER 2: Now they realize our powers. Not bad. Hey, Biri's got cash here. [26]

MESSENGER 1: Hold it. One who didn't plan on going to the Other World may be going along. *(Pointing at the* 1ST SON.) What's going on there?

MESSENGER 3: *(Pointing at the* 2ND SON.) That guy is to blame. He cooked up the phony real estate deal to make it look like the dead mother was alive.

MESSENGER 1: Is that so? *(Looking back at* MESSENGER 2.) Which code of the Other World is violated?

MESSENGER 2: It's a fabricated document in violation of Code 16, sect. 4, which deals with the boundaries between the living and dead.

MESSENGER 1: Are you sure?

MESSENGER 2: I'm positive.

MESSENGER 1: Let's go.

MESSENGER 1 & 2: Let's go! Move!

1ST SON'S WIFE: Kwaaaaak! *(Passes out.)*

The aged MOTHER *arises, opening the cover of the coffin by herself. Hopping around like a Chinese dead body, she approaches the* 1ST SON, *who is squabbling with the* 2ND SON, *and slaps his cheek. Frightened, the* 1ST SON *and the* 2ND SON *cry, "Mommy." Also fright-ened, others on stage cry, "Gramma."*

MESSENGER 2: *(To the dead body from the coffin.)* What's the matter with you, old lady? You are violating the rules.

The aged MOTHER *beckons* MESSENGER 2 *to come to her. He approaches, puts his ear near her mouth and nods his head, understanding what she said. Then,* MESSENGER 2 *steps to the* 2ND SON, *and grabs his collar. The* 2ND SON *dangles in the air.*

2ND SON: Help me!

MESSENGER 2: Listen, you! That won't do any good; your mother insists you go with her to the Other World.

2ND SON: Oh, no! I'm not the one to go there— I'm just a mourner!

MESSENGER 1: You bastard! You think you can decide if you want to go or don't want go to the Other World, like some kind of spa package tour you can cancel?

SEOK-CHUL: Is there any chance for him not to go this time?

MESSNEGER 1: No chance at all.

SEOK-CHUL *approaches* MESSENGER 1 *and whispers something in his ear. Smiling meaningfully and winking,* MESSENGER 1 *gives a sign to* MESSENGER 2 *to release the* 2ND SON, *who then falls to the floor. Now,* SEOK-CHUL *approaches him and speaks into his ear: "Cough it up now." The* 2ND SON *resists strongly at first.* SEOK-CHUL *gives up . . . The* 2ND SON, *saying nothing, rises, steps to the coffin, kneels down, and boyishly says, "Mommy." The aged* MOTHER *slaps his cheek. The* 2ND SON *begins crying "aigo, aigo," not in mourning, but as he takes the condolence money out of his pocket. When the* 2ND SON *tries to stand up, the aged* MOTHER *pushes down on his shoulders to prevent him. Then, the aged* MOTHER *talks with her hands in mime.*

MESSENGER 2: *(Translating.)* Cough up my bank notes!

The 2ND SON *takes them, along with her sealing stamp, and puts them into the coffin. The aged* MOTHER *is talking animatedly with her hands. (Mime.)*

MESSENGER 2: *(Translating.)* The certificate of title to this house, too!

1ST SON: Oh, no! Mother, please! Not the title to the house! Remember how you bought this house? This is the family home that you bought by selling rice cakes and working yourself to the bone.

The aged MOTHER *talks with her hands. (Mime.)*

MESSENGER 2: *(Translating.)* A house is not real-estate for sale. These days, people buy and sell houses or land as if they are investing in stocks and bonds; you know it's no good! A house is a house, that's it. A house is a place for relaxing comfortably, not spinning in circles lending and bribing to make money. You got that? Did I buy this house with the money earned from selling rice cakes for you to spec ulate in real-estate? Eh, for nothing? I bought this house for myself, to raise offspring in like a bird's nest, and to be revered by them when I die. If you sell this house and move to an apartment, how can I find you? If you buy an apartment, I have to get through Seoul's hellish traffic jams, wander about strange streets, and announce myself to the apartment security guard, and then, do you think I am young enough to walk up the stairs to get there? Do you?

SEOK-CHUL: There is an elevator in every apartment these days, grandma.

The aged MOTHER *talks irritably with her hands. (Mime.)*

MESSENGER 2: When the spirit is trapped in the elevator, it falls directly into hell without a trace. *(To the* 2ND *SON.)* Hurry, title to the house!

The 2ND *SON, saying "ha-ee-go," collects the title from the* 1ST *SON and throws it into the coffin.* 1ST *SON and his* WIFE *make moaning sounds and are about to faint. The aged* MOTHER *gropes in the coffin, then scatters a bunch of money in the air. Her sign language signifies her departure. (Mime.)*

MESSENGER 2: Here's some "mad' money!" Play cards 'til the cock crows. Tagga, I'm going!

The aged MOTHER *waves elatedly, while throwing the money in the air and people fight tooth and nail to pick up money, as many bills as possible. (Black out.)*

ACT V—FOR THE LIVING

People are playing cards.

1ST SON: *(Excitedly.)* What the hell? Win or lose, I call "go."
CONDOLER 3: *(Spitefully.)* You're screwed!
1ST SON: *(Eyes glaring.)* What the fuck . . . .

CONDOLER 3: Are you talking to me, your elder cousin?

1ST SON: Who cares about pedigree in a card game?

CONDOLER 3: Excuse me, you bum!

1ST SON: You're calling me a bum?

CONDOLER 3: You're the one who said who cares about pedigree in a card game.

1ST SON: All right, excuse yourself. *(To* MESSENGER 3.*)* Shuffle 'em . . . *The card game is getting hot. . . . .*

MESSENGER 1: *(Gives some cash to* MESSENGER 3.*)* It's not enough, but this is for your daily expenses. And this is for pocket money. *(To* MESSENGER 2.*)* This is for tickets, one for grandma at 50 kg. cargo, and three for us.

MESSENGER 2: Let's go higher class, this time.

MESSENGER 1: Korean Air Lines is good enough. Last time, we also took Saudi Air Lines; that was not bad, at all.

MESSENGER 2: I prefer the stewardesses on the European air lines, because they are kind and affable.

MESSENGER 1: Oh, shut up. *(Standing up and taking the rest of the money.)*

MESSENGER 2: Where are you going?

MESSENGER 1: Uh. . . I am going. . . some place.

MESSENGER 2: Some. . . place? Where, some place?

MESSENGER 1: No place special, I . . . . .

MESSENGER 2: *(Mimicking a card game.)* Over there?

MESSENGER 1: I'll clean up this time.

MESSENGER 2: Please don't do it. You're a born loser. You don't have the touch.

MESSENGER 1: This time, I can feel it.

MESSENGER 2: I am not going to take a junk air line like Saudi, which has no air conditioning, not this time.

MESSENGER 1: All right, all right. Let's take a European air line this time.

(MESSENGER 1 *approaches the card game mat.)*

2ND SON: *(Looking at* MESSENGER 1.*)* Blank check, again?

MESSENGER 1: Never mind, never mind. Keep playing, please. *(MES-SENGER 1 slyly squeezes himself in. Peeping at the* 1ST SON*'s cards.)* Forget the five matching cards and have that nil card of bush clover.

1ST SON: Why do you say that?

MESSENGER 1: What I'm trying to say is that collecting nil cards is your best bet.

1ST SON: My thought exactly. But by saying that, you just gave my hand away.

MESSENGER 1: Sorry. . . sorry. . . I blab like a woman.

CONDOLER 2: No coaching from the sidelines and place your bet.

MESSENGER 1: Oh, man, I'm embarrassed. . .

CONDOLER 2: It's O. K. as long your cash is good.

MESSENGER 1: That's all I got. I am a famous gambler from the Other World. Well—shuffle 'em.

1ST SON: Okay by me. You sucked up every bit of cash from this house and now it's time for you to cough it up.

MESSENGER 1: Well, we'll see.

2ND SON: Brother, let's take this messenger to the cleaners!

CONDOLER 1: One thousand per point, ten nil cards take all. It's Chun Doo-Whan Go-Stop game. . .

MESSENGER 1: Six matching cards rule, and "Radiant" cards are one thousand *won*, and calling "go" three times means double!

1ST SON: Shuffle 'em.

2ND SON: Die or pass out!

(As the game heats up, MESSENGER 2 furtively stands.)

MESSENGER 3: Where are you going?

MESSENGER 2: Be a lookout for me.

SEOK-CHUL: Give me some food! I can't keep mourning on an empty stomach. Where the hell is the hostess who is supposed to take care of night food?

1ST SON: Honey! Bring my friend some food, please. . . .

1ST SON'S WIFE: Coming, right way.

1ST SON: Mourning is very taxing, you know?

1ST SON'S WIFE: You're the mourner who's supposed to be taxed. What are you doing on the card game mat?

1ST SON: Playing cards is more taxing than mourning, you know.

1ST SON'S WIFE: Ai-go! Butcher and eat me.

SEOK-CHUL: Where's the food? Hurry it up, can't you?

1ST SON'S WIFE: I said kill and eat me! *(1ST SON'S WIFE exits mumbling.)*

SEOK-CHUL: *(With a big smile, SEOK-CHUL glances at MESSENGER 2. MESSENGER 2 comes face to face with him, and gives him a wicked grin.)* You want to get laid in this world?

MESSENGER 2: Uh, no, not that. Just trying to take a walk . . . .

SEOK-CHUL: I am a shaman descending three generations from my grandfathers. Tonight's horoscope is descendent in the south and the tired crescent moon makes a dim light. I recognize tonight is the night for me to be a match-maker for you and *(Looking toward the* WIDOW *sleeping off-stage.)* that shamaness. Please go in.

MESSENGER 2: Well, if you insist . . . .

SEOK-CHUL: After this night passes, I will take her who is a vagabond and make her my apprentice. As you said, it's decided that my days are numbered.

MESSENGER 2: Please arrange your human affairs roughly and come to the Other World. The Other World is not as bad as you think.

SEOK-CHUL: Since she has the spirit, I am about to make her a shamaness. What a wonderful chance it will be for her, if you have her. Please go inside.

MESSENGER 2 *goes inside and stands in front of her who is sleeping. Soon, she wakes and begins a spirit communion dance with him, their dancing silhouettes projected on the window of the room which reddens with lighting.* SEOK-CHUL'S *drum and cheering of the condolers adds to their love-making.*

(Black out.)

When the lights come up again, SEOK-CHUL'*s quiet song in Chang style is heard.*

SEOK-CHUL: Grandma, grandma—

You gave the delicious food to your kids and ate the bitter food yourself.
You made fans to get rid of mosquitoes and hunted bed bugs sitting short summer nights without complaining.
You covered up your kids with a blanket when the snowy winds blew in the winter.
 You sang your kids sound asleep with lullaby.
You made quilted pants with the best cloth to pass through the ocean wide and deep.
(Voice fades out cheerfully.) Uh-wha-dung-dung My love uh-wha-dung-dung my love.

*(*MESSENGER 3 *is alone on stage. The grand daughter,* BONG-SUK, *enters and stands in front of him.)*

BONG-SUK: Have some coffee.

MESSENGER 3: No, thank you.

BONG-SUK: Why not?

MESSENGER 3: I don't like bitter coffee,

BONG-SUK: Should I put lots of sugar in it for you?

MESSENGER 3: *(Thunderstruck.)* You trying to kill me? If I eat sugar, I will melt like a snowman.[27]

BONG-SUK: That's funny!

MESSENGER 3: This girl is trying to kill me.

BONG-SUK: Where are you taking my grandma?

MESSENGER 3: To my grandpa.

BONG-SUK: *Your* grandpa?

MESSENGER 3: Yes.

BONG-SUK: Who is your grandpa? Yama? The King of the Underworld?

MESSENGER 3: Hee heee. Everybody calls him the King of the Underworld?

BONG-SUK Mmmm. What's his name?

MESSENGER 3: Young people aren't much use these days. They forget their own grandpa's name.

BONG-SUK: That's because he died years ago. I never see him. *(Pause as she thinks.)* Got it! It's In Seok-Choe.

MESSENGER 3: That's the same name as my grandpa.

BONK SUK: You mean that's two men with same name?

MESSENGER 3: No, that's the same person.

BONG-SUK: Wow. . .so you mean my grandma is supposed to meet my grandpa?

MESSENGER 3: You might say that.

BONG-SUK: I wish I could go with her.

MESSENGER 3: Don't bother you'll be there some day, sooner or later.

BONG-SUK: Where is "there," anyway? Is it really far away?

MESSENGER 3: No, it's very near here.

BONG-SUK: Very near? Where?

MESSENGER 3: *(Poking her breast.)* Right here!

BONG-SUK: *(Frowns at him a little.)* You're strange.

MESSENGER 3: *(Embarrassed.)* No, I don't mean . . . .

BONG-SUK: To touch a lady's breast like that. . .

MESSENGER 3: I'm only telling you the truth!

BONG-SUK: Truth?

MESSENGER 3: Yeah, we are neither sent here by Yama nor going back to the Other World by taking Korean Air Lines. I was born out of your mind. I mean that I was born out of the imagination of human beings. Therefore, we're all one body and one spirit.

BONG-SUK: *(Tenderly taking* MESSENGER 3's *hand.)* You're right. We're all one spirit and one feeling because we are performing a play now.

1ST SON: *(Triumphantly.)* I cleaned up! Did I get it all?

MESSENGER 1: *(To the* 1ST SON.*)* Will you give me a cut from your take, please. *(Bitterly.)* I'll leave after the final game.

1ST SON: *(Hugging the coffin.)* Mom, I won all the money —

SEOK-CHUL: *(Suddenly standing up.)* Anyway, the world is in darkness. People, don't be saddened by thoughts of the Other World, but enjoy the time of your life, performing a *kut* as a homage to it. Then, without fear, let's go there together

EVERYONE: Eol-ssu - - -

SEOK-CHUL: *(Singing in Chang style, the chorus sung by all.)*

Don't say you have many friends; no one will go in your place. Eo-heo-ya, Eo-heo-ya.

Don't say you have many relatives; no one will go in your place. Eo-heo-ya, Eo-heo-ya.

You are buried over the mountain where pretty azaleas bloom. Eo-heo-ya, Eo-heo-ya.

Where is Paradise? That mountain in front of you is Paradise. Eo-heo-ya, Eo-heo-ya.

Everybody sings the funeral song. The aged MOTHER *rises from the coffin and joins them.*

BONG-SUK: *(Popping into the center, singing.)* "Fare thee well, fare thee well are the only words to speak."

EVERYONE: "Fare thee well, fare thee well, that's the only greeting they make."

-Finis-

NOTES:

1. In Buddhist thought, Yama is the King the Underworld, judging the souls of the newly dead.

2. A monarch of the Joseon Dynasty (ruled 1418-50), who created the Korean alphabet (*hangul*). In honor of that accomplishment, Hangul Day is celebrated in South Korea on October 9 each year.

3. A popular gathering place for the elderly to pass the time.

4. A trance ritual or performance taking many forms in N.E. Asia, led by a shaman. Contemporary Koreans, despite the country's modernity and sophistication, may consult a shaman or host a *kut* in order to insure good luck, drive out malevolent spirits, etc. In this instance, the *kut* is a device to ensure that the Mother will enter the Other World with no difficulty and be reunited blissfully with her long-dead husband.

5. The Korean government designates certain esteemed practices, buildings, or people as "cultural assets" in order to ensure proper care of buildings and artifacts and the continuation of desirable arts or other culturally important practices. The Mother may be giving Seok-Chul more importance than he actually has in order to sway her son.

6. Korea remains a highly Confucian culture, in which, according to Confucius, "rite equals right." There is an appropriate table for each important occasion and the manner in which the offerings on it are displayed has long been established in tradition. One impact of the migration of villagers into the faceless high-rise apartments in Seoul is the diminished attention to many practices formerly held inviolate.

7. During 2006, approximately 1,110 *won* equaled US$1.00.

8. Eol-ssu is a dynamic vocal response by a drummer or audience members during the performance of chanting or singing, a response designed to help the rhythm of the piece.

9. Districts to the east and southeast of Seoul, respectively.

10. The words/sounds of the shaman's chant may or may not have literal meaning in the *kut*. The Western reader may think of the un-translated passages in the script as a kind of mantra via which the shaman enters an altered state of being, becoming a vessel for the summoned spirits.

11. The *Cheonsu-kyeong* is a major canon in Korean Buddhism (*Cheon*= one thousand; *Su*= longevity; *Kyeong*=canon or classic).

12. Seok-Chul begins speaking in his own voice, but as he cries, is speaking in the Mother's voice.

13. Yeol-shee Kingdom. Yeol=ten; the ten kingdoms that make up the afterlife.

14. Koreans generally have no difficulty melding animism, Buddhism, and shaman practices; even devout Christians occasionally consult shamans.

15. *Yut* is a game traditionally associated with January celebrations. Four wooden sticks, round on one side, flat on the other, are tossed into the air. Their position after they land (round side up or flat side up) determines the number of points awarded. The points earned are transferred to a game-board and each team's "horse" advances according to the points earned.

16. "Legend's Hometown" is the title of a South Korean "soap" produced as a horror genre.

17. *Jebok* is the general designation for mourning clothes. Men's clothing (*gulkwan jebok*) consists of headgear, a hemp coat, funeral robe, belt, knee cover, traditional stockings, and straw sandals. Women's dress consists of a head rope, robe, belt, traditional stocking, and rubber shoes. Clothing for unmarried sons will vary from that worn by married men and the first son will have his own special garb.

18. Koreans rely heavily on business cards in order to determine who a person is and, thus, determine how they should behave. Education and titles are especially important information on business cards. In this case, the organizations and offices held are fictitious, designed only to impress an unknowing recipient and amuse the audience.

19. The card game is popular throughout Korea, appearing in many variations. An English translation of the cards and strategy is next to impossible within the context of this play. The cards are small, about 1.25 inches wide by 2 inches long, with flowers and animals as the dominant images, though there are some cards with human images. The game is often played with great animation, perhaps fueled by copious quantities of *soju* (rice liquor). Suffice it to say that the object is to garner more points than one's opponent and that a "Radiant" (*kwang*) card is especially valued. The Chinese character used for *kwang* means "light" or "radiance." It may be interesting in the contect of this game to note that a homophone for *kwang* means "fan" or "fanatic." The version of the game called "Chun Doo-Whan Go-Stop" is notorious for its "winner take all" rules, reflecting the syle of South Korean president, Chun Doo-Whan, during his regime, 1980-87.

20. One king of the ten who govern the afterlife. Cheongbojang is one of the two basic rhythms used in a *kut.*

21. The Korean text says that the house area is about 200 *pyeong,* a unit of measuring area, one *pyeong* equals 3.954 sq. yds. The house is sizeable.

22. Shoulder-dancing is quintessentially Korean, involving the rhythmic rising and falling of the shoulders in time with the breath. There is a kind of suspension of time and gravity when the shoulders are at their highest, a hesitation of movement with a continuation of energy and intention. Shoulder-dancing may be done upright or in a seated position.

23. The history of relations between China and Korea is long and complex, ranging from the off and on Chinese protection of Korea during the long Joseon Dynasty to the Chinese invasion of Korea in 1950. Since the 1980s, many Koreans may have looked down on China as a Third World nation. There is a South Korean saying, "The bear does the stunts, but its Chinese owner collects the money," which reflects the Korean stereotype of Chinese as slow and stingy. This view will be reflected in later dialogue revealing that Messengers from the Underground were not even given as much as a snack in appreciation for their services in Red China.

24. Gwangju is a city in South-Central South Korea, the site of a civilian uprising (in which students played a major role) against the regime of Chun Doo-Whan, May 17-27, 1980. Crack Republic of Korea troops put down the uprising with force. Outside observers estimate that 2,000 or more civilians were killed; an accurate accounting is not available. The event seems to remain an unhealed wound in the South Korean national psyche.

25. Deng (1904-1997) was known for the economic reforms he instituted during his ascendancy in the Communist Party, 1978-1992. The lines may censure Deng for the death of dissidents during his regime.

26. Biri appears to be the given name for one of the Messengers.

27. Korean superstition says that sugar will kill a Messenger from the Other World.

Introduction to *Mask of Fire:* *A Ceremony of Power*

Mask of Fire is an ambitious theatrical polemic with no characters of dramatic complexity, no characters that move from ignorance to self-knowledge out of the struggle with a situation or other characters. There are only one-dimensional symbols of aspects of humanity, none of whom (with the exception of a tribal leader and a husband and wife who are sacrificed to the fire) display any redeeming human characteristics. Yet, Lee Yun-Taek's theatrical adaptation Park Sang-Ryung's novel, *The Road to Hades*, with additional inspiration from Lee Hyung-Gi's poem, *Dream of a Parched Day on the Isle of Langerhans*,[1] is a universal allegory of the struggle between a dictator (the king) his people (the physician, the physician's wife appropriated by the king, tribal leaders, and others) and military force, symbolized by the black servant. The triangle represents the political situation in Korea at the time (the dictator surely is modeled on Korean president, Park Jung-Hee, assassinated in 1979, who had a reputation for sexual excesses), but the play's context and content may well be applied to many nations and regimes around the globe in the present day.

The script's storyline is straightforward: A prince kills his hedonistic father and usurps the throne in order to revolutionize the nation. A melting furnace, a kiln, becomes a symbol of purity, into which human sacrifices are thrown in a Dragon Fire rite, the dragon being an ancient East Asian symbol of fertility and wisdom, but most especially of rain. To subjugate the people and deal with a long-term drought, the king decides to control his people with opium, planning a production monopoly to fill the government treasury. The physician tries to use his reason and knowledge to end the king's madness, but the physician himself is flawed by jealousy toward the king, which bends knowledge toward madness. So he invents an ingenious way of infecting the king with syphilis, which also infects the doctor, his wife, and the black servant. At the close of the play, the Chief Lady-in Waiting is left holding the young orphan of two unfortunate commoners earlier sacrificed to the kiln, her eyes "little by little glow with madness."

The play's structure is linear, without complexity and without sub-plots, as titles of the play's episodes suggest:

1. A Dream of a Parched Day on the Isle of Langerhans
2. A Strong Power Needs a Scape-Human
3. Warped Knowledge Dreams of a Revolution
4. If a Flower of Ignorance Is Able to Cover This World
5. From the History of Sex to the History of Madness
6. The "Weaponization" of Knowledge

Lee utilizes "prototype, ritual, . . and social language of reason" [2] and, indeed, the core actions (revenge, sexual excess, and murder) are forwarded by prototype and ritual—not character development. Recall that Lee is not interested in theatre realism; symbols thus are central in his work. The Isles of Langerhans is a part of pancreas, thus the cancer seen in a large hanging x-ray at the play's opening is symbolic of the cancer infecting the entire nation (Korea) and the Western reader must bear in mind that, even after 1988–89 and the relaxation of censorship laws, free and open criticism of the South Korean government could be a dangerous undertaking. Presidential power and the intimidating omni-presence of riot squads and military units continued to limit the people's role in South Korea's experiment with democracy. The stabbing of the tribal elder in Episode 4 is a symbol of the fate met by many who opposed the government in the 1970s and '80s. (See the ending of *Citizen K* for a similar depiction.)

The central symbol in the play, the furnace or kiln, has a kind of womb-like shape, and thus may be seen variously as a symbol of Mother Earth, the sun's energy, Korea's extraordinary rise as an industrial power, and, prototypically, purification of evil spirits (some masks used in mask dance drama are ritually burned after performances even today). The critic, Kim Mi-Do suggests yet another symbolism not evidenced in the script, but used in the performance. In the final scene, Yeo-Ok (the Female Jailor) dons the "Mask of Fire" and begins to dance like a shaman, accompanied by a traditional Korean song, *Gujiga* (Song Welcoming the Divine Lord), sung for King Suro (first century CE). The song refers to a turtle (representing sacrifice and a phallus) and to the turtle's head (the king). Fire, in this interpretation, symbolizes inflamed female sexual desire and Yeo-Ok falls into the fire at the moment of her orgasm. [3]

Orgasm in *Mask of Fire* and the frank staging of sexual activity by the noted director, Chae Yun-Il (1947–), earned the 1993 production at the Sanullim Theatre the nickname, the "stripping play." Lee's work attacks political and social taboos at the time (recall his reputation as a "cultural guerilla"), and Chae's direction did not soften the sexual implications in the play. The resulting nudity and violent sex was viewed either as a serious artistic attempt to break down traditional Confucian stoicism, or as commercial erotic opportunism. Certainly, the production gained much notoriety (no doubt benefiting box office receipts at the same time it altered the Sanullim theatre's long-time image as a producer of intimate, realistic works). Lines such as "open your foul pussy" from Episode Three and the action in Episode Six when the Female Jailor copulates with the Physician while he is handcuffed may well be true to Lee's stated intention to shake audience stereotypes, but one may question the *thematic* necessity of their visual enactment.

There *are*, however, two important themes from Lee's earlier *Citizen K* that are reprised in *Mask of Fire*. First is the vacillation of so-called learned men about moral choices. The Court Physician in *Mask of Fire* sounds much like Citizen K when he says: "Learned men like me . . . would choose if possible not to die for any cause." The second theme is that of opportunistic women who deny their avowed love for a given man in order to curry favor with a more powerful man or force, as the Female Reporter perjures herself to accuse Citizen K and the Female Jailor runs to the King to tattle on her husband.

Lee's bold theatre imagination and reliance on images, rather than realistic dialogue resulting from complex psychology and particular personalities, has been noted elsewhere. *Mask of Fire* and *The Dummy Bride* are two "ceremony" plays featuring infants in core images. Two women promise to nurture the babes, the Bride because the child will be the world's hope, the Lady-in-Waiting because she "is the mother of this island." Both babes represent a new generation, saviors of modern Korea, promises of a better life—or they may be yet another sham hope and a potentially self-serving messiah or dictator. Lee's stage direction ending *The Mask of Fire* provides no clue: "Only the sound of a metal bell remains on the empty stage, telling of the end of an age." Is the new age to come one of hope—or one of futile repetition of old corruptions? Lee may have written elsewhere about what he intended, but the ending of the play itself does not bring his earlier arguments to a clear conclusion. And that may be exactly the result Lee intended.

The critic, Yoo Min-young found *Mask of Fire* incomplete, raw, wordy.[4] Lee's tendency in *Mask of Fire* is to explain, to lecture, rather than dramatize; it is Lee speaking through each stereotypic character, rather than characters speaking for themselves. Reading some speeches can be like reading the records of a debate. Still, it is difficult to ignore Lee's powerful, theatrical imagery and his passionate convictions in this ambitious work. In the hands of a skilled director and actors who can bring some humanity to the major roles, so that we as an audience may empathize with them—we don't have to *sympathize* with them—Lee's work may well appeal to audiences outside of Korea. His investigation of madness versus reason remains universal and postmodern tendencies in the theatre today may be well employed to illuminate the fractured images of madness in the play. *Mask of Fire*, whatever its characteristics, remains an important event in Lee Yun-Taek's artistic development and a milestone in the contemporary Korean theatre.

NOTES:

1   Park Sangryung (1940-) lived in Vancouver, Canada for thirty years, writing in Korean, focusing on the nature of death and spiritual enlightenment. *Road to Hades* (Yeolmyeong-gil) was published in 1986. The poet, Lee Hyung-Gi (1933–2005), it is interesting to note, had pancreatic cancer centered in the Isles of Langerhans.

2. Mi-Do Kim. "Dynamics of Power and Madness," in *Laugh, Beat Drums, Die* (Utta, Bukchida, Jukda), ed. Yun-Taek Lee (Seoul: Pyeongmin-sa, 1997) 257–264.

3. ——

4. Min-Yeong Yu. "Experimental Drama of a Dictator's Madness," in *Laugh, Beat Drums, Die* (Utta, Bukchida, Jukda), ed. Yun-Taek Lee (Seoul: Pyeongmin-sa, 1997) 267–268.

Mask of Fire: A Ceremony of Power

Dramatis Personae:

Elder King, father to the King

King

Court Physician, son-in-law to the Chief Lady-in-Waiting and the Elder King

Female Jailer, wife to the Court Physician, daughter to the Chief Lady-in-Waiting, step-sister to the King

Black Servant

Chief Lady-in-Waiting, step-mother to the King

Elderly Cabinet Minister

Male Escapee *(doubles in the role of a minister)*

Female Escapee *(doubles in the role of a minister)*

1. A DREAM OF A PARCHED DAY ON THE ISLE OF LANGERHANS

Langerhans—an island of chaos.
The stage looks like a gaunt human body, a bag of bones.
The Isle of Langerhans is the name of a human organ, part of the pancreas. When something abnormal occurs in this island, the human gets diabetes, with excessive urine flow. Therefore, the stage is a landscape of a sick person's internal organs.
The lungs are hardened like lead with cells of cancer,
Blood vessels are entangled like black ink,

Leukocytes are eaten by germs, creating white splotches here and there. This abstract, expressionistic painting is used as arras in front of the bed. Moaning from the bed.

Uh . . . . uh . . . . uhhuh . . . . huhuhu . . . . uhuh . . . . uhuhuh

A man lying on the bed stretches his hand up to pull the rope above.

Daaaahng—

The metallic sound of a bell spreads through the air.
The ELDER KING rises upon that tolling, which sounds like the end of the century.
His expressionless face is devastated from opium addiction.
He stares into space with no focus.
Saliva drools from his unclosed lips.
With the echoing sound of the bell, the KING enters,
accompanied by the COURT PHYSICIAN, who is holding a medical bag.

ELDER KING: The entire fortune I have saved (*Pointing under the bed.*) is here . . . . . . *under the . . . bed.*

The KING takes several steps to the ELDER KING and kneels down. He stretches his hand under the bed and pulls out a large urn.. Looking into it, suddenly, he makes eye contact with the ELDER KING.

ELDER KING: You . . . take them all. (*The KING stands and turns away; the ELDER KING grabs one of the KING's shoulders.*)

With a grimace, the KING tries to ignore him, but the rake-like hand of the ELDER KING grips him even more tightly.

ELDER KING: Please . . .

The COURT PHYSICIAN takes a hypodermic syringe from his medical bag and opens a drug bottle. The ELDER KING gazes at the drug bottle with enraptured eyes. At this moment, the KING removes his shoulder from the ELDER KING's grip.

ELDER KING: (Rolling up his shirt sleeve.) Would you inject me . . . here, please?

The COURT PHYSICIAN *approaches the* ELDER KING.
The ELDER KING *hands the urn to a servant.*
The COURT PHYSICIAN *holds up the* ELDER KING*'s arm to inject the drug.*

ELDER KING: Hurry, hur . . . ry . . . up. Shoot me with that drug . . .

At the very moment the COURT PHYSICIAN *tries to inject the* ELDER KING, *the* KING *interrupts, grabbing the* PHYSICIAN*'s wrist.*
The COURT PHYSICIAN *and the* ELDER KING *look at the* KING.
The KING *snatches the syringe from the* COURT PHYSICIAN*'s hand, and moves to center stage. He then sprays the injection into the air.*

ELDER KING: You . . . son-of-a-bitch.

Lights dim on the stage with the desperate sound of the ELDER KING. *A heavy sound of the metal bell. As the sound of the bell dies away, the body of the* ELDER KING *is seen suspended above the bed. He has hung himself.*
As the lights come up full,
the KING, COURT PHYSICIAN, CHIEF LADY-IN-WAITING, *and a few* COURTIERS *hurry in.*

CHIEF LADY-IN-WAITING: Oh, no . . . *(Running to his body.)* a great king . . . .

The KING *intercepts her, and covers the dead body of the* ELDER KING *with a white sheet. While the* CHIEF LADY-IN-WAITING *sobs with her hand over her mouth, the* KING *looks around at the* COURT PHYSI-CIAN *and* COURTIERS *with a cold smile on his lips.*

KING: We'll skip the needless ceremonial funeral for him. There's no need for moving drums and mournful hymns. We need six men to carry the coffin, and a funeral leader. That's enough. Anyhow, this is the end of his age. The quicker, the better.
BLACK SERVANT: *(A huzzah.)* Prepare the inauguration of the young king! A new age has dawned!
KING: *(Interrupting him.)* We don't need an empty ceremonial inaugura-tion. We disdain the people's cheers. This island is on the edge of bank-ruptcy. *(Pointing at the* COURTIERS.) From you courtiers down to ten year-old school boys, nobody expects anything from the government.

Yes, I know it. *(Coldly smiling towards the audience.)* You *(Pointing at the stage.)* increasingly do not trust this government. *(Pointing at several places among the audience.)* There is hostility and the energy of insurrection everywhere. The entire responsibility for this, however, *(Pointing at the white sheet)* is over there. Look, the past is gone, hanging itself into history. One age is over now. *(Stops swaying and folds his hands behind his back.)* I now, coincidently . . . am standing at the center of a new history *(Looking around)* like this. *(Laughing.)* Yes, this is a coincidence. I coincidently have the good fortune to be a king now. *(To the* BLACK SERVANT*)* You there, crown me!

The BLACK SERVANT *brings a shabby crown and puts it on the* KING's *head.*

The KING *looks up at the crown, a frown on his face,*

KING: This is far too small for me! Why?

BLACK SERVANT: There was no time for me to size it, Sire.

KING: It doesn't matter. *(Wearing his crown, he brightens. Shoulders held high in pride, he smiles at the audience.)* I am a king. *(Pause.)* Why is that? *(Pause.)* Because I was born the son of the Elder King. It's by chance that a man is born from a queen's womb. So be it, since I was born the son of the old king, I am supposed to be a king, so to speak. How absurd and unfair this world is! *(To the* COURTIERS.*)* It's a fact of life, isn't it? The man born the son of a billionaire is supposed to be another billionaire. The only way for the poor to be rich is robbery or fraud, isn't it? *(To the* COURT PHYSICIAN.*)* From whom did you learn your profession?

COURT PHYSICIAN: The Great Court Physician who was my father taught me.

KING: See? Even knowledge and medical skill get handed down like a fortune. But it is not an achievement. It's just chance, chance! We're surrounded within a world controlled by chance. *(Taking off the crown, and looking at it.)* I got this crown by chance. *(Flings off the crown with no hesitation.)* I don't like chance. The thing you get by chance is not the real power of a real man.

COURT PHYSICIAN: Even if you get it by chance, man has the ability to alter chance into the inevitable, a logical consequence.

KING: Yes, that's correct!

COURT PHYSICIAN: That is a capacity of knowledge.

KING: That is a capacity of power. Knowledge has no power to transform chance into an inevitable outcome. Knowledge is . . . *(A frown on his face.)* What is your profession?

COURT PHYSICIAN: Pardon me?

KING: What do you do for living?

COURT PHYSICIAN: I am the court physician, Sire.

KING: So, your job is to take care of the King's health, and assess peo
ple's mental health using your sizeable intellect.

COURT PHYSICIAN: *(Humiliated.)* Yes, Sire.

KING: That is called knowledge.

COURT PHYSICIAN: But, even if the knowledge itself has no power,
it guides the power to the appropriate ends.

KING: Yes, I understand you, generally. So, your family has held a
physician position in our court for four generations. When I was a boy,
I used to be taught by your father that knowledge guides power in difficult times. Now, so that you record new history noting the specific
meanings of it, I'm going to use that knowledge.

The KING *strikes the fireless metal furnace twice with his fist.*

The sound of heavy percussion, followed by the BLACK SERVANT,
who wears a "Mask of Fire." He holds a metal chair for the new
KING. *With a fierce glare, he steps towards center stage and places
the chair there in precise movements, like a military officer. The* KING
sits with satisfaction.

KING: *(To the* BLACK SERVANT.*)* You were entrusted with the defense of the outer areas of this island under the condition that the government cares for your parents and children. One might say your life
has been monotonous, looking out at the endless horizon over the sea,
your skin scorched by the salt sea-wind. Your muscles rusted inside,
and your head filled up with nameless birds' shit, becoming fossilized.
But you, a black servant, even if you steadfastly defend this island,
your patriotism will be useless because the core of this island is rotting. Do you understand what I'm saying?

The BLACK SERVANT *grins.*

KING: My father, our old king, used to embrace the treasures and power
he pillaged at the Dead Sea, thirsting after every kind of sensual pleasure. How bored he must have been on this battle-less and unchang-
ing island! But, our old king had no wits to use his copious time
wisely. At best, his decadent state was one of indulgence in a vague
haze of pussy and opium. *(In a loud voice.)* Who *did* invent that drug,
anyway?

COURT PHYSICIAN: *(In an embarrassing situation.)* Yes, my father . . .

KING: Then, your father as good as killed the Elder King. That drug drove him into degradation little by little, destroying flesh and spirit.

COURT PHYSICIAN: The old king specifically ordered the preparation of that drug; he used it at *his* request!

KING: You son-of-a-bitch, what is your knowledge for? Yes, there was the Elder King's special order, but, you are a man of profound learning on this island and manufactured a great deal of opium even though, reasonably, you knew it was wrong!

COURT PHYSICIAN: Don't you know the bloody character of the old king? Those who refused his order were killed.

KING: I see. . . To survive himself, your father murdered the hero of an age. But my father was also a man who could sense your father's insidious inner thoughts. That's why your father died early.

LADY-IN-WAITING: Please choose your words carefully, Sire. The Great Court Physician died in ill health.

KING: You, aunt, do not defend the Great Court Physician any longer! The Elder King became aware that the pleasure addictive drug prescribed by the Great Court Physician was sapping his life force. And for that reason, the Great Court Physician poisoned him.

LADY-IN-WAITING: That's baseless rumor. For the sake of the new order on this island, I want no more troubling discord. Let bygones be bygones and keep an open mind when dealing with affairs of state.

KING: Now, I am more transparent than ever. I have grown up watching with my own two eyes the whole process of the corruption of this island, in which spread a cancer. *(Striking the metal chair.)* How I longed for, waited for this moment! Why? Your own eyes will see the reason, immediately! *(To the* BLACK SERVANT.*)* Proclaim martial law.

BLACK SERVANT: *(Standing menacingly at center stage.)* Henceforward, taxes for this new government will be placed in the national treasury to be divided into equal portions for the King and ten ministers. These ten ministers will receive monthly payments according to their rank and salary classification, to be decided by the King.

KING: In other words, this nation is not a publicly held corporation. *(Pointing at the auditorium.)* You, the elder ministers, have corrupted this island hanging on to your vested interests but doing nothing. *(Waving his hand.)* Not any more.

BLACK SERVANT: *(Looking around the auditorium while smiling radiantly.)* Any objections? *(Pause.)* Next, we proclaim today a new National Founding Day . . .[1]

LADY-IN-WAITING: That's impossible.

KING: Stay out of this, Aunt . . .

LADY-IN-WAITING: The kingship of this island has been held by our family, by that Court Physician's family extending back for four generations, and by the families of ten major ministers. *(Sharply.)* It's not the King's personal property.

KING: To speak frankly, Aunt. This island belongs neither to the royal family, nor to the Court Physician's family, nor to those ministers who are vested with all powers, nor to village heads and so forth. It also belongs to those people who face absolute poverty and cannot free themselves from public welfare.

COURT PHYSICIAN: Then your Excellency's martial law is really a resolve to reform the government for the sake of those people?

KING: And if it is?

COURT PHYSICIAN: *(Kneeling)* Then, I will obey your decision.

KING: In a sense, today is a new National Founding Day and the Memorial Day for the Revolution.

LADY-IN-WAITING: The Revolution?

KING: Yes. Don't you know that? I am not a successor to the crown. I grabbed the crown with my own two hands.

LADY-IN-WAITING: This is treason!

BLACK SERVANT: Martial Law: Code 3. "All people shall conduct the Fire Dragon ceremony in order to pray for everlasting peace and the stability of the National Founding Day and the Memorial Day proclaimed this day." All you people, come here, to the furnace!

The KING *stands up from the metal chair, and draws a white arras. The dead body of the* OLD KING *is carried away, and a sturdy new metal furnace appears. On the back arras hang Masks of Fire, symbols of might. The* BLACK SERVANT *hands a Mask of Fire to all. The* KING *dons his mask first. Then, everyone, some hesitating, gathers at the furnace, respectfully putting on the Mask of Fire. But, The* FEMALE JAILER, *not yet donning her mask, bravely raises a question.*

FEMALE JAILER: This comical furnace is our god which we are supposed to worship? . . .
It's nothing but a blob of metal!

KING: It is. This furnace is merely a hunk of metal as you see. But this metal object is fabricated from an indigenous mineral, this island's sole iron ore, mined and smelted here. This is the very resource to feed this island. The very resource.

FEMALE JAILER: Are we supposed to bow to the resource?

KING: Yes. How great a resource this is! I am not going to worship some formless idol. I will devote myself to a useful material I can see with my own eyes. This metal resource is our national religion from now on.

COURT PHYSICIAN: Then neighboring nations will sneer at you for practicing idolatry.

KING: Don't make me laugh. What do we care about neighboring countries? We must reunite the scattered minds of the people. This furnace will be the new hope of this island, and it will create a new mythology. What is special about this mythology? We can make it in this way: this new Fire Dragon mythology will save us, manifesting itself as an transcendent language dominating the spirit of this island, amending corrupt public morality and settling public unrest.

FEMALE JAILER: But it would still be silly to worship the metal thing, wouldn't it, brother?[2]

LADY-IN-WAITING: How dare you call the King a brother?

KING: It's all right, Aunt. I can't help being a kid in front of this gorgeous girl. *(Caressing her gently.)* You are May Queen of this island as well as a cousin on my mother's side. I will apprentice you to a female shaman devoted to the Fire Dragon rite.

FEMALE JAILER: Over my dead body. I don't want to spend my youth by this metal contraption. I want to marry . . .

KING: Marry?

FEMALE JAILER: Yes. *(Presumptuously pointing at the* COURT PHYSICIAN.) I want to marry him.

The COURT PHYSICIAN *turns his face away abruptly.*

FEMALE JAILER: *(Approaching him.)* What? Don't you love me? *(The* COURT PHYSICIAN *is perplexed.)*

KING: *(With gusto.)* Good, everything is good today! Let's celebrate your wedding tonight, worshipping in the first Fire Dragon rite.

BLACK SERVANT: Martial Law: Code 4. All political offenders will be released today in order to proclaim the National Founding Day and Memorial Day of Revolution. *(Brings the large urn which is filled with the* ELDER KING's *treasures.)* Return this illegal profiteering to the people.

Cheerful percussive festival music with a light metal-bell sound.
The Fire Dragon flares up in mysterious colors. A drum sound is heard from afar.

A servant brings a cage in which are several pigeons.
The KING *takes one pigeon out of it.*

KING: *(Reciting)* Oh, barren soil. Oh, blighted, forsaken island on which half-ripe heads of buckwheat droop. I am dreaming. Of a scorched-black sky. Bless us with rain on this parched, dust-covered earth. *(The* KING *puts a pigeon into the furnace.)*

The FEMALE JAILOR *is frightened and screams.*
The drum sound becomes louder, and the flames are reflected in the KING's *eyes.*

2. A STRONG POWER NEEDS A SCAPE-HUMAN

The clock says five thirty in the morning.
In front of the furnace, the COURT PHYSICIAN *ponders,*
walking slowly toward, and talking to, the audience.

COURT PHYSICIAN: It takes almost an hour and a half for the fire in the furnace to glow. Today is seventh anniversary of the Memorial Day of Revolution, an annual event. Very early in the morning, when the old King hung himself from his own bed, the young King ignited a fire in this furnace, unused for a long time. From that time on began a firing up of the furnace once a year at that same moment, the same early hour. *(Turning to the furnace.)* This furnace is made of metal, the ore dug from the mine and presented to the King by laborers. It was placed on the old King's bed, functioning as a kind of heater during chilly winter days.[3] *(With a bitter smile.)* This practical utility has become this island's religion through the young King's capricious imagination. *(Gently touching the furnace.)* This cold, hard, metallic object has become the religion on this island. But this religion frightens people. *(Pause.)* I remember the very day when a pigeon was thrown into the fire of this furnace seven years ago. My wife screamed in terror. She was then the kind of person who felt sorry for and feared the death of a pigeon. My wife . . . now keeps on dancing even if a living person is thrown into that fire . . . So evil! *(Tone changing into a confession.)* I am at best an ineffectual scholar. I have read numberless books, and I am very proud of myself as one who mastered science and healing arts. But what kind of power can my learning assert in a violent world? The King's lunacy and imagination surpass my erudition. It is certain that the King has a psychological affinity for the fire.

I can't tell whether he is a fire-worshipper or is a kind of love-deprived psychotic, fascinated with the furnace as a substitute womb. In the beginning, the King created a beautiful symbol by throwing a pigeon into the furnace, proclaiming that this pigeon would be reborn as a mystic incense delivering our prayers to Heaven. At that time, it was a kind of scapegoat ceremony. Three years ago, a couple of goats were delivered into the fire by King's own hand. After that, for three days and nights, a disgusting stench befouled the entire island. We tried to understand his actions as the hysteria of a King suffering through continuous drought year after year.

I am a scholar. A scientist. A court physician. I have no interest in politics. *(Sighing.)* The King worked tirelessly to restore order on the island and to create national wealth. But his revolutionary strategies were severely unfortunate. Drought. Yes. The drought lasting for three years must have over-stimulated the King's imagination. That drought drove good-natured people into savagery, and allowed the older generation to use its vested rights in treasonous rebellion.

That's true. Power is dependent upon, moved by, materialism. Although mythology and religion and like things guide the human spirit, our living is dependent on the economy. *(Lifting up the mask and waving it. His voice becomes impassioned.)* I don't believe in this mask. Power isn't sustained by covering each person's opinions with this mask. I don't trust the King's imagination that tries to govern this world in this way. I am a socio-scientist. My logical, socio-scientific grasp of things is the power to sustain this world. Keep your eyes open! You'll see how the King who tries to govern this world with nonsense such as mythology and the power of the imagination tumbles down! *(With assuredness.)* Then, who is the right man for this island? The right one's true self will emerge sooner or later. The elder ministers have again begun to compete for supremacy. They try to secede with their tribes. Bit by bit, the King's power to govern shrinks. If this island becomes anarchic, the King will use a potent remedy. He needs a human scapegoat. The ministers who dream of treason and betrayal will be it. Those who first try sneak away from this island to the continent will be the scapegoat.

Along with the ominous sound of a drum, a metal bell rings six times. Enter the KING *with his* daughter, *the* CHIEF LADY-IN-WAITING, *and the* BLACK SERVANT, *the* SERVANT *holding a rope that drags in a couple, one male, one female.*
The KING *ignites the fire in the Fire Dragon.*

The BLACK SERVANT *makes the couple kneel at the altar behind the Fire Dragon. They have the look of death on their faces.*

MALE ESCAPEE: Your Majesty. . . No! My Lord. I boarded the boat in order to buy a pack of herbal medicine for my wife, who was ill after giving birth. This is true! To where could I escape, leaving my wife and new born baby? Pl . . . please let me go. *(The KING blankly looks down at him.)* I can't even feed my wife a bowl of brown seaweed soup![4] *(He cries pitifully.)*

FEMALE ESCAPEE: *(Seeing the COURT PHYSICIAN.)* Your Honor, please let us go. Please petition the King for my husband. If we both are executed, who will care for our new born baby? Please, I beg of you, save my husband . . .

COURT PHYSICIAN: *(Rushing to the KING to seek mercy for the couple.)* Your Majesty, I fear that this kind of Fire Dragon ceremony will bring curses down on our heads instead of blessings. Please stop!

KING: You are kindhearted but foolish. Don't you know that pity or sympathy harm social order and prosperity on our island?

COURT PHYSICIAN: Your Majesty, please desist! You shouldn't do this to these innocents.

KING: I am a fire, and a will of fire. This island is maintained by the energy from this furnace. We have to burn away the lives of those who attempt to escape this island. Doctor, if, from God's grace, you truly want a downpour of long-awaited rains on this island, do not criticize me.

COURT PHYSICIAN: Your Majesty, life ends when we die. There is only that, leaving behind no flame to worship. A life is the ultimate thing, and the foundation of fire. Is there not a difference between life and fire? In my opinion, what you are doing is wrong, contrary to the purpose of life.

KING: Eunuch with a big mouth— be quiet!

COURT PHYSICIAN: *(His complexion reddening.)* I beg your pardon?

KING: What use are you learned men? I, as King, do my best twenty-four hours each day to govern this island. What? This is contrary to the purpose of life? You gutless sop! If that is so, then try it yourself! Govern this island with your own hands. You can't rule according to some theory in a book!

The COURT PHYSICIAN flees the room in humiliation. The ESCAPEE couple kneeling in front of the KING look at him with entreating faces.

KING: *(Looking down at them and pointing at the furnace.)* Get in there, move!

ESCAPEES: Spare us! Be merciful, please spare us!

KING: *(With a heavy sigh, looking at the* BLACK SERVANT.*)* Take them.

The BLACK SERVANT *takes them by the hands to the furnace. The couple embrace and weep. The* CHIEF LADY-IN-WAITING *steps forward to gaze on the horrific scene with an expressionless face. The* KING *strides behind the furnace and voices an incantation like a founder of a religion, the intoxicated sounds somewhat like those of a poet.*

KING: Oh, muse of omnipotent fire! Our bodies are but a spark from a bonfire, and this place is merely a stagnant pool in which we stay only briefly. Before some misfortune strikes because we weak mortals don't attend thee, our long-enduring god, in thanks for numberless, merest sips of water, please give us rain! Rain!

In desperation, the FEMALE ESCAPEE *hands the baby in her arms over to the* CHIEF LADY-IN-WAITING, *who tightly grasps the baby. The* BLACK SERVANT *lifts the man up and throws him into the furnace.*
The drum sound intensifies.
A woman's screams.

KING: Farewell, scapegoats. Rain will come from your sacrifice.

The FEMALE ESCAPEE *spits into the* KING's *face.*
The BLACK SERVANT *lifts her up and throws her into the furnace.*
Screams.
The KING *wipes his face with the back of his hand, then bursts into unmanly tears.*

3. WARPED KNOWLEDGE DREAMS OF A REVOLUTION.

A simple bed sits in front of a black screen.
The COURT PHYSICIAN *lies on some books instead of a pillow.*
This is his room.

Enter the FEMALE JAILER, *a haggard figure.*

COURT PHYSICIAN: What is it?

FEMALE JAILER: His Majesty sent me to see you, saying that you're more precious friend than this island . . . He also said that he would generously overlook your rudeness at the altar today.

COURT PHYSICIAN: How is my mother-in-law? I heard she fainted.

FEMALE JAILER: She'll be fine.

COURT PHYSICIAN: No, she isn't. Where on this island is there anyone living in sound spirits? *(Clutching at his heart.)* Uhhhmm.....Uhhhhmmm.

FEMALE JAILER: Is something wrong with your heart?

COURT PHYSICIAN: Go away and leave me alone!

FEMALE JAILER: You don't think of me as a friend any more.

COURT PHYSICIAN: From the very beginning, you were a gift from the King. You're an opiate. *(Caressing her chin.)* Giving me this living opium, the King planned to dampen the fire in my body. He planned to dominate this island using that insane, barbarous crucible, holding my knowledge as a slave. Yes, he takes it all! He placed the Black Servant ahead of me, deprived me of my rights and took his ministers' lands. But, now, Your Majesty, now you must contend with nature. How about going a few rain-dry rounds with cursings and mirages under scorching sunlight, undergoing the agonies of a long drought which reminds you of the greatness of nature. That omnipotent furnace, the weapon born of your imagination, will be powerless from this day forward.

FEMALE JAILER: Take it easy.

COURT PHYSICIAN: *(Agitated.)* Oh, the King sent you to me, you said. For what? To find out whether or not I'm a eunuch? Let me see, let me see, now. Maybe you've just finished fucking with the King, right? Tell me the truth. You weren't a virgin when you married me. Some bestial thing wore out your pussy. When I recognized that it was the King, I became a cripple. *(Louder.)* Yes, I am a eun . . . uch!

FEMALE JAILER: *(Sobbing.)* I am afraid of living.

COURT PHYSICIAN: *(Throwing her down on the bed, and sitting astride her)* Well! Reality check! *(Pulling up her skirt.)* Open your foul pussy! Take in my crippled dick. Let me ram that lifeless pussy the King fucked out, feeding you opium! If this is a game for him, let's play it!

(The FEMALE JAILER *thrusts him away in shame.)*

COURT PHYSICIAN: I take it you don't need me any more? *(With murderous intent.)* But the key is still in my hands. *(Lower voice.)* You know what I mean? *(Louder.)* In my hands!

FEMALE JAILER: Calm down, please! I will get off this island . . . .

COURT PHYSICIAN: *(Grabbing her wrist.)* Not a chance! I don't want to offer you up as a sacrifice in his insane fire game. You have been a flower on this island from the beginning. A most useful flower, you know. The King *(Caressing her.)* has made good use of this flower. You satisfied his sexual appetite, while he handed you around as an opiate to keep my mouth shut.

FEMALE JAILER: No. It was I that chose you!

COURT PHYSICIAN: *(Embracing her tightly.)* Yes, it was you who chose me. The King just used your choice. I knew that. Thus I forgave you and loved you.

FEMALE JAILER: And I'm grateful, my darling.

COURT PHYSICIAN: But I don't know whether you love me or not.

FEMALE JAILER: *(Peevishly.)* I love you, love you, love you. You were the one I chose. You were the one I . . .

COURT PHYSICIAN: *(Stopping her mouth with his hand.)* Thank you. *(Pause.)* Then, let's use our love as a weapon.

FEMALE JAILER: What?

COURT PHYSICIAN: The union of your love and mine can be a weapon, the only way we can heal this fire-crazed island.

FEMALE JAILER: I don't follow you.

COURT PHYSICIAN: *(Strongly in a lower voice.)* A revolution.

FEMALE JAILER: Revolution?

COURT PHYSICIAN: Yes, revolution!

FEMALE JAILER: You're just a scholar. You have no power!

COURT PHYSICIAN: I came to live with that exact thought. No, my entire family would have lived that way. I am a scholar! I have no power! *(Pause.)* Dragged as we were to this island by the King who was the supreme pirate throughout the Dead Sea, my family's knowledge was a defeated, crippled scholarship from the very beginning. Ever since my family settled on this island, we have been captives of a nation created by pirating and built on the knowledge of the captured. *(Chuckling.)* A nation founded on the knowledge of thieves and hostages — how absurd is its history! From the very beginning the ruling power luxuriated in thievery and dictatorship, and knowledge was subordinated, with the inferiority of a hostage. Damn it, how tragic this combination of this power and knowledge is, driving this island into endless chaos and violence. Knowledge degraded into subservience of a ruling power. In any case, both have a responsibility for the situation. Now it's time for payback!

FEMALE JAILER: What are you going to do? You. . . frighten me.

COURT PHYSICIAN: I will take your love as a weapon. *(Strongly in a lower voice.)* Turning knowledge into a weapon. Understand? At last,

little by little, I see the realities of this world. Why my father produced
opium, and why he jotted down various secret potions in his note-
book, scientific ways of poisoning, and how to cultivate venomous
germs . . .

FEMALE JAILER: You're thinking of poisoning the King, aren't
you?

COURT PHYSICIAN: Yes, I am.

FEMALE JAILER: Since the old King died, all food and drugs must be
tested by the Chief Lady-in-Waiting before the King tastes them. My
mother will die first.

COURT PHYSICIAN: I know that.

FEMALE JAILER: And?

COURT PHYSICIAN: Orgeat syrup. [5]

FEMALE JAILER: What are you talking about?

(Enter the CHIEF LADY-IN-WAITING, *holding a baby in a quilt.)*

FEMALE JAILER: Mother!

COURT PHYSICIAN: Mother-in-law, what's that baby?

LADY-IN-WAITING: It's beautiful, isn't it?

FEMALE JAILER: Yes, it's beautiful.

LADY-IN-WAITING: It's the child of the couple who were sacrificed
today.

COURT PHYSICIAN: I see.

FEMALE JAILER: If the King becomes aware this, there will be hell to
pay.

LADY-IN-WAITING: The King is a human being; he cannot tell me
what to do. The King *(Looking down at the quilt.)* grew up sucking at
my breast like this. His mother was burnt at the stake for eloping with
a sailor, and I *(Rocking the baby.)* raised him with my own hands . . .
The ungrateful. . .

FEMALE JAILER: What brings you here?

LADY-IN-WAITING: The King has just now proclaimed the promotion
of opium cultivation.

COURT PHYSICIAN: What?

LADY-IN-WAITING: He will order opium cultivation, turning it into a
government business like tobacco and ginseng.

COURT PHYSICIAN: I can't believe what I'm hearing . . .

LADY-IN-WAITING: You must stop him. No matter the cost, you are
the only one who can stand up to him. Go and stop him. The aged cabinet minister is appealing to him now.

COURT PHYSICIAN: Now, he goes too far.

Black out.

4. IF A FLOWER OF IGNORANCE
IS ABLE TO COVER THIS WORLD . . . .

A black curtain opens.
The Isles of Langerhans are stained with dark blood as before.
The KING is seated on a metal chair,
an AGED CABINET MINISTER kneeling before the KING,
pleading with him.
When the COURT PHYSICIAN enters,
the BLACK SERVANT stops him.

KING: *(In an ice-cold tone.)* So?

MINISTER: Please rescind the opium proclamation, Your Majesty. The people should not be experimental subjects!

KING: More than seventy percent of the entire product will not be sold in the domestic market. Didn't I say that it will be cultivated for export?

MINISTER: Even less than thirty percent of it would be fatal to the public health, and when our island becomes notorious for exporting opium, we will be isolated by our neighbor nations.

KING: How many times have I told you, idiot? For domestic sales, "For your health, smoke wisely" will be inserted on each case of opium, and what do you mean by "international isolation"? Though most countries put up a good front, mouthing "for the peace of all mankind," "for mutual prosperity," etc., as a matter of fact, they are dealing with all kinds of dirty business behind the scenes. This is the main way of diplomacy these days. It's because this island is full of your kind of idiots that we are still a poor country, isn't it?!

MINISTER: Please moderate your words, Your Majesty!

KING: I beg your pardon? What did you say?

MINISTER: *(Rising before the KING and glaring.)* You've lost the people's faith in your leadership. I tried not to provoke unrest among the people, however, my patience is at an end. *(In a loud voice.)* Civil war! Our seven villages in the south-east are already prepared to take the field against you. If I do not return to them, they will wage war immediately and occupy the capital within three days.

KING: You jest. Even if you do not return to them, your villages cannot mobilize for war. You dolt! Do you think anyone can usurp my reign? Your kind of naïve rebellion will topple me? Don't make me laugh! The rabble in those seven villages is dispersed now, bad-mouthing each other. The leaders already are captured and being brought to the

capital. Do you understand? Why don't you half-wits straight-for-
wardly just ask for your share of the profits? How dare you mouth
concern for the "public health"? *(Slaps the* MINISTER's *face, then
orders the* BLACK SERVANT.*)* You, take away this useless relic!
MINISTER: *(Dumb-struck.)* What . . .
BLACK SERVANT: Come here. *(The* BLACK SERVANT *grabs the*
AGED CABINET MINISTER's *hair.)*
MINISTER: Save me, please . . .

The BLACK SERVANT *stabs him with a bayonet.*
Enter the COURT PHYSICIAN, *in consternation.*

KING: You're here. I was about to summon you. What do you think of
my plan?
COURT PHYSICIAN: To what do you refer, Your Majesty?
KING: I'm talking about opium production. This new plan for economic
development is superb, isn't it, offering some beautiful illusion to
people care-worn by a life full of petty concerns.
COURT PHYSICIAN: *(Ironically.)* It will keep people in line and take
care of all complaints about economic crisis and governmental
tyranny.
KING: Moreover, it will be a basic means to solve the unemployment
problem. . .
COURT PHYSICIAN: It will be a regular source to fill national treasury. *(Stealing a glance at the body of the* AGED CABINET MINIS-
TER.*)* As the stream of decentralization becomes stronger day by day,
monopolizing the cultivation of the opium to centralize economic
profit and political influence can build a powerful government.
KING: *(Now sensing the* PHYSICIAN's *irony.)* What are you saying?
COURT PHYSICIAN: It's an excellent idea, Your Majesty. But, there
are problems: the average span of human life on this island will be re-
duced by more than ten years, and sanatoriums for the insane and isolation asylums for the dregs of society must be expanded remarkably.
Moreover, we must consider the increase in sex crimes and moral corruption.
KING: You oppose the plan?
COURT PHYSICIAN: *(Glancing at the* BLACK SERVANT.*)* I don't
want that butcher of human beings cutting my throat with his bayonet,
not yet. I want to live if I can. Even if the life would be that of a puppet and not my own, I would want to live. What do you think of that,
Your Majesty? It would be nice to survive enjoying something.

KING: That's true.

COURT PHYSICIAN: Learned men, like me, who live by selling shallow knowledge, would choose if possible not to die for any cause, would live in disgrace, even though the world could become a paradise if he just risked his life.

KING: You're grown up, at last.

COURT PHYSICIAN: *(In a lower voice.)* But, in fact, there are times when even a man like me really wants to die for once. I'm not sure, but perhaps that's why I would want to live.

KING: Man dies only once, anyway. If you don't have traitorous ideas like the old minister's, I will appoint you Secretary General of the Bureau of Opium. This is your opportunity to move into a position of power and out of the powerless chair of knowledge.

COURT PHYSICIAN: *(Perfunctorily.)* Thank you, Your Majesty.

KING: In fact, this business was a long-cherished dream of the old king and your father, wasn't it? Your father produced opium and the old king, passionate about that business, consumed it himself, like a mouse in a lab. Now, let's make our fathers' dream come true!

COURT PHYSICIAN: But, first and foremost, the minimum fatal dosage should be determined in order to prevent a catastrophe.

KING: Ten opium farms spread over the island will be developed and controlled by you, then the entire crop is to be sold to the government only. This plan will not permit any individual expenditures for opium.

COURT PHYSICIAN: A law only is not sufficient. Stronger controls are needed.

KING: Of course, a police network and a special oversight team will be put into operation. But, alas, what hardships would be good for me to visit upon those who try to pilfer some opium at their own risk? But. . . they are not a problem. Opium sold to the government will be manufactured into cigarettes in the factory under your control. Dried hemp leaves will be coated with liquid opium, then rolled and sealed up with real tobacco leaves.

COURT PHYSICIAN: You draw a perfect picture without me, Your Majesty.

KING: Where opium is concerned, my ideas are as good as yours. I conduct research and scholarly study, too, you know.

COURT PHYSICIAN: As needed, Your Majesty.

KING: Indeed. I don't give a damn for any knowledge that is not practical. *(Pause.)* By the way, have you not thought about manufacturing an aphrodisiac?

COURT PHYSICIAN: An aphrodisiac, Your Majesty?

KING: Yes, an aphrodisiac.

COURT PHYSICIAN: There is some available on our island. I made it just to get pigs to copulate.

KING: I don't believe it! Can a king use the same thing as a pig? Make an especially strong dose for me.

COURT PHYSICIAN: As a matter of fact, the one for copulating pigs is the strongest. . .

KING: These days, I can't get it up . . .

COURT PHYSICIAN: Too much drugs, Your Majesty.

KING: Do something for me, will you?

COURT PHYSICIAN: Fear not, Your Majesty. *(Nodding lightly, the* COURT PHYSICIAN *heads off-stage. Just before exiting, he stops and speaks under his breath.)* Yes, I will make the strongest one for you, so strong you can't sleep the whole night through.

Exit the COURT PHYSICIAN, *and black out.*

Scene 5 begins with the slow beating of a drum.

5. FROM THE HISTORY OF SEX
TO THE HISTORY OF MADNESS

A heavy drum sound in the dark;
the KING *pants for breath, and the* FEMALE JAILER *moans.*
In between the KING'*s panting, he curses occasionally.*

KING: *(Heard in the dark)* Huhhgg . . . huhugg . . . This, son-of-a-bitch . . . huggg . . . Damn . . . Kill him . . . kill . . . hugg . . . huhhgg . . . I'll kill him . . . tear out his legs . . . hugg . . . legs . . .

Lights up slowly, and the KING'*s bed is shown.*
The KING *is on top of the* FEMALE JAILER, *copulating.*
He then gets out of bed, half-naked, in extreme anger.

KING: The Court Physician! Go and get him. Now!

Putting her clothes on, the FEMALE JAILER *leisurely exits the room.*

KING: *(Putting his clothes on distractedly.)* That bastard, I will . . . that unfaithful bastard . . . *(Hitting his head in a near tantrum.)* Aaack!

What a half-wit I am!! *(Taking a deep breath.)* I am nearly dead! *(Taking a deep breath.)* Let me see, this son-of-a-bitch, how should I kill . . . boom . . .

The COURT PHYSICIAN *is brought on, grasped by the nape of his neck by the* BLACK SERVANT, *who has the* PHYSICIAN *kneel by kicking him in the shins. The* KING *watches him intently without speaking.*

KING: *(Gesturing with his finger.)* Come over here. *(The* COURT PHYSICIAN *goes calmly on his knees to the* KING.*)*You tried to kill me?

COURT PHYSICIAN: *(Grinning.)* How did you know?

KING: Isn't it obvious? *(Pause.)* By the way, you used a low form of address to me.[6]

COURT PHYSICIAN: What difference does it make? I'm going to be executed anyway.

KING: *(Calmly.)* Why did you do that?

COURT PHYSICIAN: What . . .

KING: If I died like this *(Twisting his own neck).* you'd be satisfied?

COURT PHYSICIAN: You humiliated me. . . calling me an eunuch . . .

KING: So you tried to poison me?

COURT PHYSICIAN: *(Pause.)* I never did that.

KING: *(Pause.)* Ha! This son-of-a-bitch is lying to my face. *(Pointing upwards.)* Aren't you afraid of retribution?

COURT PHYSICIAN: *(Gazing up at the heavens.)* Why would I futilely lie to you at this very moment? I've never tried to poison the King.

KING: Then you mean your wife is a liar?

COURT PHYSICIAN: *(Sneering.)* My wife? She tattles too quickly. What a faithful woman she is!!

KING: Too quickly?

COURT PHYSICIAN: I told her that I would kill you some day if I could.

KING: Then, to kill me is your hope?

COURT PHYSICIAN: We all are cancer tissues that should be killed some day, aren't we? The world doesn't change because of power-hungry scholars like us, don't you think?

KING: *(Striking the* PHYSICIAN *on his head.)* If you want to die, be my guest! *(Kicking him.)* You unfaithful, two-faced bastard! It's my failing that I thought of you as a life-long pal with whom I swam naked when I was a kid on this island. . .

COURT PHYSICIAN: They were the good old days. I really don't understand why man becomes ugly as he ages.

KING: That's a research problem you must dwell on until the time of your next sacrificial rites. *(To the* BLACK SERVANT.*)* Throw him into a dungeon. He will be the next scapegoat for the Fire Dragon rite!

The BLACK SERVANT *picks up the* COURT PHYSICIAN, *wrenching his back.*

COURT PHYSICIAN: Ow! Take it easy, you butcher!

KING: Hold it! Didn't you really put poison into that aphrodisiac?

COURT PHYSICIAN: I said I didn't. . . Does it work?

KING: Well, it's extraordinary, indeed. But, why didn't you put some poison into it?

COURT PHYSICIAN: Why should I do such a stupid thing? You'd certainly test it on somebody else before you'd take it.

KING: Of course. *(Pointing at the* BLACK SERVANT.*)* He tested it first.

COURT PHYSICIAN: See, what did I tell you?

KING: Do you have any last request?

COURT PHYSICIAN: Are you going to honor it?

KING: Anything except that I must die . . . *(Pause.)* . . . You've been my friend, though.

COURT PHYSICIAN: I want to see my wife.

KING: For what? To kill her for tattling to me?

COURT PHYSICIAN: *(Shaking his head.)* She belonged to the King, from the beginning. I don't want to dispute that vested right. I only . . .

KING: Only what?

COURT PHYSICIAN: Because of the jealousy and anger I felt towards you, I've never slept with her properly. I want to sleep with her.

KING: You crazy bastard, trying to get everything you can when it's time to die.

COURT PHYSICIAN: It's no big deal to you, is it? You offered her once as a beast-like slave. What do you care for her!

KING: All right . . . After checking with her, I will allow you to do it as long as her safety is guaranteed.

COURT PHYSICIAN: Thank you.

KING: What's a friend for? This is it.
(The COURT PHYSICIAN *is taken out.*
Alone, the KING *momentarily sinks into thought. Then. . .)*

KING: Now that your husband is on his way to the dungeon, come out here.

(The FEMALE JAILER *approaches him from the bed behind.*

She crouches down beside him and leans towards him.) Who the hell are you? Where are you come from?

FEMALE JAILER: What?

KING: I've known you since you were a toddler. But what I really don't understand is what makes human beings tick. What kind of person are you?

FEMALE JAILER: I really don't know.

KING: *(Gloomily.)* You're right. Your answer sounds correct. You don't know the answer and I don't know it either. The fact that we don't know it frightens us and sows seeds of distrust. *(Pause.)* So people are lonely creatures. *(Pause.)* Do you love me?

FEMALE JAILER: *(Pause.)* I really don't know.

KING: Did you love the Court Physician?

FEMALE JAILER: . . . .

KING: Speak to me. Did you love him?

(The FEMALE JAILER *nods silently in assent.)*

KING: *(Confused.)* If that's so, then, why, why did you inform on him?

FEMALE JAILER: *(Slowly.)* You asked me to report on everything he said and even his behavior.

KING: So you ratted on the husband you loved?

FEMALE JAILER: *(Fiercely.)* You asked me to report him, didn't you!

KING: To report him to me is more important than to love him?

FEMALE JAILER: *(Hysterically.)* I don't know! I really don't know! Something in my blood, not my will, drives me to do it. You're to blame for these things!

KING: I know. . . I sometimes have felt from deep within unnamed urges strong enough to foment revolution and conquest. They are not shallow emotions of fragile humanity, like love and happiness. They are darker and stronger than anything, a certain madness clinging at the bottom of men's hearts. From long before now, I've been repressed by this madness which can't be named. It drives me mad, and occasionally leads me commit unimaginable brutality, without hesitation, without remorse. I wonder if some kind of fiery specter wandering in the universe flies to me on this island like a nightmare. What is it? Is it a hero? God? Or a ghost of the devil who stands opposed to God. No, I believe that is a man. Isn't it man's innate temperament, lying coiled somewhere in his breast? *(Pointing at the x-ray of the Isles of Langerhans which shows white spots in the black-colored background.)* Take a look at this. This is the interior of this island on which we live. Everything is becoming corrupted, and white corpuscles are slowly invaded by dead blood-fluids and inflammation. The same as the very moment the old king was dying. Now this forebodes the time when the demise of one brief generation is at hand. *(Loudly.)* But I do not fear such an advent! Why is that? This is the essence of life. The history of man has been maintained by the continuing drama of decay while ulcerating and putrefying into pus. Life is ugly by nature. When ugly, worn-out life itself seems beautiful, man can be saved. The Court Physician! That son-of-a-bitch doesn't understand. What he suggests is at best invisible repairs of portions of reality. Then he brags on himself arguing "this is a reformation," or "this is peace." *(Pointing at the inner part of the Isles of Langerhans.)* Take a look. From where can we put our hands to work, ameliorating this hopelessness?! At most, the only thing that those so-called heroes can do is demonstrate their despair as they wallow in the mud. *(Shaking his head and collapsing into the throne.)* Why am I weak and sweating? When I'm done ramming women, more sleepless despondency approaches, biding its time. Ah, melancholy time, my body is stiff like lead. My muscles become rusty, and my spirit is withered by mouse-like time. *(Lifting his body.)* What am I hearing? This island sinking down just like I do? Some sound echoing up from Atlantis sunk deep into the ocean? Is it a bell-sound? Or a bird singing? Is this the hammering sound in a man's chest? Or is this the sighing of ghosts buried in a field of brown seaweed?!

A sound from afar, which is like a mouthed sound from the depths of the heart, and like a sharp, metallic sound from a stringed instrument. Lights out slowly.[7]

6. THE WEAPONIZATION OF KNOWLEDGE.

A dungeon.
The COURT PHYSICIAN *is sitting on the floor with his arms handcuffed behind.*
With a boom, the door is opened, and the FEMALE JAILER *enters. Her face is wooden as she stands before the* COURT PHYSICIAN, *without feelings of guilt or fear.*

COURT PHYSICIAN: Come in, my cute opiate! Hurry, unfold the drama of dissembling and vicious double-crossing! If you came here to listen to my last wishes, remove these pants with your virtuous hands. Hurry, undress me! Good, loosen my belt first *(Wriggling his hips.)*, undress me at once! You are a virtuous woman, indeed. I begin to understand you, little by little. Once I thought of you as a whore, and ground my teeth with indignation. But I was wrong. I'm beginning to think that you may be the only human ever born on this island. The only human being beyond the reach of great learning and authority, the human being reborn as a most beautiful animal!

The FEMALE JAILER *is sits astride his body with an absent expression. She begins to undulate her body sullenly.*

COURT PHYSICIAN: *(Who has climaxed.)* How was it? I am not a eunuch, am I? No, I could be a eunuch. But not now! Why you ask? Through will power and spirit accumulated throughout my entire life, I have hardened up my crippled penis, confirming that imagination is able to transform into real power. I recover my self-confidence, like this . . . *(Lifting his hips.)* I can spurt up my cum— like this!
(The FEMALE JAILER *sexually enflames, little by little.)*
COURT PHYSICIAN: *(Thrusting his body upwards.)* Shall we chat? Now, it's your turn to tattle to me, hmmm? Now we merge our flesh. We are united in one body. You can tell on the King now. How is he? What is he doing?
FEMALE JAILER: He is sick.
COURT PHYSICIAN: In what way?
FEMALE JAILER: He talks in his sleep . . . I think he is growing mad bit by bit.
COURT PHYSICIAN: Shall I give you more specifics? He likely hears sounds in his head, bursts into a violent cold sweat, and grows weak. He may hallucinate frequently, seeing mirages. . . *(FEMALE JAILER, with some dreadful thought, stops her sexual writhing.)* There will be not only physical symptoms, more deadly mental symptoms, as well. He will descend without seeming cause into deep despair and weakness, and will start dreaming of suicide . . . *(FEMALE JAILER stands.)* But I will not take him far enough to commit suicide. I will give him a fatal blow with my scientific reckoning! My science!
FEMALE JAILER: *(In a pathetic voice.)* You did use a poison!
COURT PHYSICIAN: Orgeat syrup! You were careless in your tattling to the King. Because of your ignorance. Since you didn't know what orgeat syrup was, you were not able to report it to him correctly. Oh, well! Even if you understood, what difference would it have made? The King could never even conceive it. He's stupid to be a king! Orgeat syrup! That was written in my great grandfather's diary. A

transparent liquid with no color, no smell, no poison. Since it has no poison, no color, and no smell by itself, it can pass the screening process. The King has eaten meals and drunk water laced with orgeat syrup. Of course, others ingested it, too. But this orgeat syrup is a smart chemical which doesn't do any harm to man by itself. When the King took aphrodisiacs, the orgeat syrup started working. Haahaahaa! From the moment those aphrodisiacs for pigs entered the King's body, and his whole body began to burn with sexual desire, the orgeat syrup took effect, working to freeze his body. That's its natural feature. *(Greatly delighted.)* The quicksilver spreads in the King's body. His guts are filled with the cold ice of the quicksilver! Haaahaaahaaa! *(FEMALE JAILER hastily dresses and runs out.)* Go on, tattle to him all you like. But it is I who holds the key! Now is not the time for us to die, neither the King nor me! Little by little his spirit will be destroyed and he himself will witness it!

With a tense drum sound, the lights slowly fade to black.
When the lights come up, an inside wall in a clear dark-blue color is seen.
The COURT PHYSICIAN *kneels on the floor, bound.*
The KING *stares at him intently. The* BLACK SERVANT *is not his former self, now standing dispiritedly.*

KING: I am well informed of what you have said. Now it is time for you to use the power of your learning to show me a way to cleanse my body.
COURT PHYSICIAN: Nothing could be simpler.
KING: Is it? Wonderful! Give me an antidote now with no more trickery!
COURT PHYSICIAN: *(Looking down at the rope around his body.)* Don't play games with me, Your Majesty. Please untie me
KING: If I release you, will you flee this island?
COURT PHYSICIAN: *(Shaking his head)* I will not go anywhere.
KING: Even if I would kill you?
COURT PHYSICIAN: I believe your word is good.
KING: Then we have a deal. But, you are confined to your lab. *(To the* BLACK SERVANT.*)* Release him. *(The* BLACK SERVANT *releases him.)*
COURT PHYSICIAN: *(Rubbing his wrists.)* When you drink ionized water, the quicksilver will be neutralized. We call that a kind of chemical reaction.
KING: Ionized water?
COURT PHYSICIAN: Don't eat any food for a couple of days, drink a barrel of sea water a day . . .

KING: *(Confused.)* Is it that simple?

COURT PHYSICIAN: Knowledge is power. Science is composed of simple principles.

KING: You smart-ass bastard! *(Trembling.)* Your learned brain will burst some day— like a watermelon!

COURT PHYSICIAN: *(Bowing lightly.)* Bear in mind that some day your power can have unpredictable, disastrous consequences.

Exit the COURT PHYSICIAN *in quick short steps.*

Black out. . . a drum sound..

At the end of the drum sound, a sharp metallic sound is heard, followed by the FEMALE JAILER's *scream.*

7. MYTHOLOGY OF THE ORIGIN OF FIRE— ARSONISTS OF THE WORLD.

The KING *and* FEMALE JAILOR *spring out of bed half-naked, swollen blue spots on their bodies.*

KING: Wha . . . what is this . . .

FEMALE JAILER: Oh . . .

KING: Is anybody there? Anybody . . . *(Enter the* BLACK SERVANT, *with plodding steps. On his body there are many swollen spots.)* I . . . I can't believe my eyes . . .

(The BLACK SERVANT *falls on his knees. He is dying.)* That, that son-of-a- biiiiitch— Court Physician! Come out here and answer to my sword!

The KING's *hand trembles as it grasps a sword.*
Enter the COURT PHYSICIAN.
He stands like a picture in front of the KING.
There are blue spots on the COURT PHYSICIAN's *body, too.*

KING: You have it, too.

COURT PHYSICIAN: Yes, Your Majesty.

KING: Why? Why did you do these . . .

COURT PHYSICIAN: I told you once that I wished to die. Do you remember that?

KING: Yes, you told me that, for the intelligent man, not to die was shameful, if by his sacrifice the world could become a paradise!

COURT PHYSICIAN: Yes, Your Majesty. That was the biggest hurdle for me as a man.

KING: I don't want to hear it! I'll permit no more blasphemy of my reign! I want a de-tox formula now!

COURT PHYSICIAN: . . .

KING: Get moving!

COURT PHYSICIAN: There isn't any!

KING: What?!

COURT PHYSICIAN: It was a cultivated syphilis. There's no way to flush it from our systems. Our guts and flesh are corrupted already and will decompose without leaving a trace. How can anyone recover the skulls that will dissolve into nothingness?

KING: You sneaking rat! You destroy us with a poison from your learning. Should your so-called learning help destroy mankind in this way and thus destroy our nation?

COURT PHYSICIAN: I didn't destroy anybody. *(Pointing at the* FEMALE JAILER.*)* That woman did.

KING: I can't believe it!

COURT PHYSICIAN: The syphilis was cultivated in my body and I contaminated that daughter of this island. Like dandelion seeds, the cursing message spread. *(Pointing at the* KING.*)* You who have abused political power for private gain, *(Pointing at the* BLACK SERVANT.*)* that puppet soldier! *(Sighing.)* And my knowledge, too. Now, it is time for us to fade into history. My father and I lived with political power, and struggled against it, and, in the end, met despair.

KING: *(Lamenting.)* You idiot! You don't understand how the world turns! The end of it is already prepared. It comes just a bit early. But the time, yes, the splendid feeling of accelerating time is vital! It can't be helped! Let's prepare a Fire Dragon ceremony.

COURT PHYSICIAN: The memorial day of the revolution is months away, yet.

KING: Today is a new memorial day of the revolution. *(Firing up the furnace.)* This day you give me will be recorded as another memorial day of the revolution.

The KING *climbs to the altar and kneels down, joined by the* COURT PHYSICIAN *who has removed his upper body clothing. The* BLACK SERVANT *steps back furtively, then, in a flash, comes undone, collapsing. The* FEMALE JAILER *kneels down, crying.*

COURT PHYSICIAN: Dear King, my old friend, I send you back to Mother Nature in this way. Please take me with you as a token of friendship.

KING: *(Rather dispassionately.)* You're right, we were friends.

COURT PHYSICIAN: *(In a conversational tone.)* I feel sorry for you as a man, but I couldn't stop your madness any other way.

KING: You idiot. You destroy me too early. Because of you, this island will brim over with chronic deficits, irregularities and corruption.

COURT PHYSICIAN: How is that?

KING: Those ministers who survive will do anything for their own profits, and this island will revert to a reactionary time. It is certain that people freed of tension just play and eat with no thought for tomorrow. My aunt, the poor thing, will raise motherless children, again. Even though one of them becomes the new hope for this island, who knows if a learned blockhead like you with some conscience will jump at the chance to poison him again, and everything goes backward. That's the way of the world. There is no hope in this kind of world. *(Strikes the* COURT PHYSICAN's *head in anger.)* How could you cut short my business for nothing, you fool—

COURT PHYSICIAN: What was your business? You tried to rule this world at your whim, making people get high on opium, didn't you?!

KING: Yeah, that was it, exactly.

COURT PHYSICIAN: Hmm. . . There was no way I could permit that. I am a weakling, but I am a learned man. There is a conscience in this cage-like heart, and my reason's eyes are opening wide. Even though a world of chaos comes, the innocent spirit will prevail. You're judged now in the name of justice.

KING: Why is it that righteous, virtuous men always win? When a man like me steps forward to play a dirty role, why don't you help, rather than interfere? You pinhead! What is the result? Presumably, men in this world will reconcile and forgive each other in order to maintain the status quo, a vicious cycle of history. There is no progress in that kind of world. *(Sighing and looking at the furnace.)* Oh, fire! Through your power, I would dispose of every womb, every gut on this rotting island! I wished that only those with strong muscles would survive to swim over that green coral sea, then to see a new world and encounter new people. *(Raising both hands feebly.)* Oh, fire, you are the incarnation of despair. When we should despair, we must know how to despair completely. I have lived for despair. *(Shaking his head, he drops his hands and looks at the* COURT PHYSICIAN.*)* Why is it that fire becomes a religion, a mythology? The last day of Pompeii. ended with fire, and Revelation says that this world should be baptized with fire. The only power that can purify this world is fire. A fire! Cry out, "fire," you son-of-a-bitch. Every sleeping puppy will spring up and start barking, and those who are selfish will flee the house in bare feet. *(Crying.)* I would like to be an arsonist. I would like to destroy this world, this chaotic world, by fire five minutes before its end. Then will there be a deluge . . . the tale of Noah's ark begins and with that a new history will be inaugurated, a new history before my eyes . . . I am dead . . . Everything goes wrong . . . goes wrong . . .

The KING *tumbles down into the furnace.*
The COURT PHYSICIAN, *stunned, is alone looking into the bowels of the furnace.*
Then he haltingly half-stands, finally standing up and coming down the stairs.
The FEMALE JAILER, *dumbstruck, looks at him out of the corner of her eye.*
The COURT PHYSICIAN *takes a syringe from his pocket quickly, and, rolling up his sleeves, tries to inject himself. But he drops the syringe, sapped of energy. The syringe rolls over to the* FEMALE JAILER, *who looks at it. The* COURT PHYSICIAN *thrusts his arm out at her urgently.*

COURT PHYSICIAN: Time's up. Shoot me now, come on . . .
FEMALE JAILER: *(Picking up the syringe.)* What is this injection for?
COURT PHYSICIAN: Hurry up! My skull's calcium is liquefying. Shoot me now to harden it again! Even though I become a cripple with polio I must live.[8] We must live, no matter what! Fire is nothing. It's no worse than a medicine to expel a tape-worm, is it? Or like a diarrheic. When the world needs a vermifuge, or when you feel bloated, take some pills, lunatic, instead of burning it. *(Thrusting his arm.)* Now, shoot me up, now, hurry! *(The* FEMALE JAILOR *picks up the syringe and injects the dose into the air.)*
COURT PHYSICIAN: *(Yelling desperately)* Are you crazy? What are you doing?
FEMALE JAILER: *(Standing up like a ghost . . . goes up the stairs to the furnace.)*
COURT PHYSICIAN: *(Following her.)* No, don't do it!

The FEMALE JAILER *dons the Mask of Fire hanging behind the furnace. She looks very coquettish with the mask on her face.*

She picks up a fire brand to make the flame stronger.
Flaring up with the flame,
the FEMALE JAILER *falls into the furnace as though she were danc-*
ing.
The COURT PHYSICIAN *drops to his knees, stupefied.*
Enter the CHIEF LADY-IN-WAITING, *holding a baby in a blanket.*
She places the baby on the empty KING's *bed.*
Then, with full strength, she pulls the rope suspended from above.
A metal bell sounds clearly.
The COURT PHYSICIAN *staggers his feet to approach the baby.*
He tries to choke the baby with his clawed hands.
The CHIEF LADY-IN-WAITING *forcefully shoves him away,*
sending the COURT PHYSICIAN *to center stage.*

CHIEF LADY-IN-WAITING: Don't touch this baby. It is he who will
rise to govern this island.

COURT PHYSICIAN: That baby . . . will be an arsonist. He will harm
this world!

CHIEF LADY-IN-WAITING: *(Smiling icily.)* I must nurture this baby,
because I am the mother of this island. If you will not serve him, *(Cru-*
elly pointing to the auditorium.) swim across that ocean, if you have
the courage.

The COURT PHYSICIAN, *with despairing eyes, turns his head to*
look out at the endless ocean.
The CHIEF LADY-IN-WAITING *pulls the rope with full strength.*
The metal bell keeps sounding.
As the eyes of the CHIEF LADY-IN-WAITING *little by little glow with*
madness, the lights fade to black.
Only the sound of a metal bell remains on the empty stage, telling of
the end of an age.

-Finis-

NOTES:

1. National Foundation Day is celebrated in Korea on October 3, marking the traditional founding of Korea by Tan-gun in 2333 BCE.

2. The Korean text uses the word, "oppa," or brother, but the word does not neces-
sarily denote a blood relation. In this case, she uses a familial, endearing term that di-
minishes the King's rank and authority.

3. There seems to be an inconstancy in the text here. The furnace-kiln is large enough to burn a human, yet the author tells us that it was once used as a kind of foot-warmer for the Elder King's bed.

4. Seaweed soup is highly nutritious and should be in great supply on the island, but the drought and the man's poverty conjoin to render him powerless to help his ailing wife.

5. True orgeat syrup is made from almonds, sugar, and rose water or orange-flower water and used as a base for many alcoholic cocktails. Here the term is used to denote a tasteless, colorless ingredient that interacts with other chemicals to infect the King.

6. The Korean language has many levels of politeness, each used depending upon the relationship between those communicating. In this instance, the Physician should have used language that lowered his own status and elevated that of the King, but, instead, he spoke in familiar, rather than exalting, terms, thus insulting the King.

7. The interested reader may wish to compare this stage direction with that at the close of Anton Chekhov's *The Cherry Orchard*.

8. The Physician confessed to poisoning the King with mercury (false confession) and with syphilis (the truth). He mentions polio here, not because he in fact has polio, but to make a point about the depth of his need to live—*even* if he had polio.

Introduction to the *Dummy Bride:*
A Ceremony of Love

The Dummy Bride was written roughly five years after the Seoul Olympics, an event symbolizing for many Koreans the nation's transformation from a third world country with one of the lowest standards of living on the globe into an economic power in Asia. Often referred to as the "miracle on the Han River," the "miracle" was the result of aggressive government economic priorities, advantageous relationships between major Korean conglomerates (*chaebol*) and the government, important trade agreements with Japan, industrious tenacity and hard work of the Korean people, and, it must be noted, the infusion of millions of U.S. dollars in direct aid and military paychecks, most especially during the Vietnam War. Seemingly overnight, but in fact over decades, South Korea became a consumer nation, no longer an agrarian society, but one fueled by industry, with one of the world's highest annual growth rates. But, like the United States and Japan earlier, and China in recent years, rapid industrial growth transformed South Korean society. The tide of migration of Korean farmers to Seoul eroded former connections to the land, village life, age-old beliefs and traditional values. Unrestrained industrialization without concern for labor laws or humane working conditions for workers led to illness, injury or death (see Park Kwang-Su's 1995 film, *A Single Spark*) and the environment was blighted by foul water and even dirtier air. While South Korean government agencies and the populace in general now have taken steps to keep Korea green, *The Dummy Bride* remains an apt parable of a materialistic modern society adrift without core values as the 1990s approached, indicting a society that—in Lee's writings—honored false religious and political prophets. Its relevance to Korean life has not lessened in the twenty years since the play was penned.

Set outside of the Shindorim station in southwest Seoul, a short train ride away is the infamous Kuro Industrial Complex, the locale of Park Chong-Weon's 1980 film, *Kuro Arirang*, a scathing indictment of a system that abused workers in inhumane conditions in the rush to capitalistic economic advancement. "Shindorim" may mean "New City Sylvania," but the playwright clearly uses the title here satirically and it is no accident that the action takes place around a train station at dusk, as night creatures begin to emerge from the underground. Prostitutes, the blind, beggars, police on the "take," a drunken professor, a jobless young man, an over-educated, but ineffective political activist, a sham religious messiah—these representations of the under-belly of the Korean economic "miracle" did not benefit from the "boom." They are the "sinners" who populate Lee's parable.

The opening of the play is lyrical, both in the quality of the music used ("Like a Bridge over Troubled Water") and the dialogue itself. The opening exchange between Michael, the young beggar, and his dad, the Blind Singer, suggests that the action about to unfold is a dream:

Michael: Dad!
Blind Singer: What?
Micheal: I dream every night.
Blind Singer: What dream?
Micheal: The Dummy Bride riding in a white sail boat is coming through that dark sky. . . .
Blind Singer: The Dummy Bride is dead.
Micheal: My dream isn't dead.

When the Dummy Bride pulls her vending stall on stage, a train whistle blows, some denizens enter, and a coin is tossed into Micheal's begging cup. The play's prelude concludes, and the night's fantastical events begin. In a sense, Micheal's dream is brought to life, becoming increasingly nightmarish as the play unfolds.

Lee Yun-Taek's storyline is straightforward: customers gather at the stall and, with libido fueled by alcohol and loneliness, descend into orgiastic dancing, during which the Dummy Bride is impregnated, only to hang herself, for none of the men involved will accept responsibility. Nevertheless, the Bride appears in a final *tableau vivant*, holding a statue of a child with open eyes, and freeing the denizens of their sins.

The Dummy Bride manifests multiple aspects of Lee's theatrical vision. First, the Korean title, *Pabo-kashi*, means "stupid bride," most literally. However, metaphorically the *pabo* involves word-play in English translation: "dumb-y bride" and "dummy bride." In Lee's production, the bride was in fact a miniature dummy/puppet, attached to a living actress, thus precluding any audience identification with realism. The paradox, of course, is that the "dummy bride" comprehends life and its pain more deeply and poignantly than any other "character" in the play. Significantly, in stark contrast to the raw sex evidenced in *Citizen K* and *The Mask of Fire*, the use of puppets and masks in *The Dummy Bride* creates rather grotesque, certainly unreal, images of sexual orgy.

As night deepens and liquor-fueled libidos drive behavior, the aura of bacchanal is heightened by the appearance of a fantastic music box, complete with dancing puppets (performed, in fact, by actors) into whose mouths coins are placed in order for the music of the night to continue. A sham messiah preaches a message of salvation as though he were a performer in a circus sideshow and, in profound despair, the Patriotic Young Man, once so secure in his belief that he could save Korea from itself, commits suicide. Lee's nihilistic view of modern life is manifested in a brief scene between the Blind Singer, Michael and the Dummy Bride:

Blind Singer: Who are you? Are you a dummy?

(She keeps silent.)

Michael: Where do you come from?
Dummy Bride: *(Pointing at the night sky.)* Over—there.
Michael: *(Looking at the above.)* Over where?
Dummy Bride: The first town under the sky.
Michael: The first town under the sky? You're not supposed to be here. Here is not a good place for you to live.
Dummy Bride: I will live here.
Blind Singer: Here things are out of joint. The world has no center.
Dummy Bride: I will live here anyway. I will produce a baby, who will grow as it should be in nature. I will put hope in my baby.
Michael: It's no good for you to produce a baby. The world is being defiled by degrees, becoming a colossal dumping ground. Then, what becomes of the babies in this world? Education will be useless to them. And there would be no adults to lead them. The babies will turn out wild and crude and think only of themselves. They will be buried in a dumping ground, fighting each other.

The denizens of the area don masks representing the faceless uniformity of Korean life—or the masks behind which regimented, repressed Korean civil behavior is freed of restraint and given over to bestial desires. Surely, the music and dancing leads to orgiastic (religious?) ecstasy and, in a dance with the Police Sergeant, the Drunk, and the Jobless Young Man, the Dummy Bride loses her innocence and her virginity. Michael's warning that it is no good to produce a baby takes on a deeper level as the Bride "at last has a liaison with the flesh and blood of this strange world" and she "accepts the harsh realities of her situation, robbed of her innate nature, her virginity spoiled."

Now begins the most difficult section of Lee's play. The Bride from the beginning of the play has been performed by an actress with a three-quarter scale puppet attached her front. Now, as the Jobless Young Man rushes off to get medicine for the Bride's tummy-ache (she is pregnant), a scene begins in which foot-puppets are used, masks placed on the feet of the actors. Lee's use of foot masks here illuminates more than any other aspect of his work in *The Dummy Bride* the centrality of image and sheer physical energy in his theatre. The foot masks — and the huge tooth that falls to the stage earlier — remind the reader and audience that surface realism is not a goal in Lee's work. He employs startling, seemingly unconnected images (such as the tooth), physically aggressive staging, unpredictable changes in emotion (especially comedy in the midst of unpleasant moments), incongruous mixtures of grating, harsh sounds and the most poignant folk music to reach his audience. Traditional Korean theatre, which features both puppets and masks, remains familiar to audiences and Lee relies on that familiarity to connect with audiences in an instinctively cultural, rather than an intellectual literary way. The use of dummies, most especially when the Dummy Bride hangs herself, also creates a grotesque beauty and theatricalism not possible with a living actor, as the dummy lies truly lifeless yet vibrant with artistic possibilities.

The concluding scenes in the play constitute a "passion play." The Messiah drags in a crucifix, hangs himself after conducting "the last Mass on this planet" and ascends to Heaven. The Christian imagery is not misplaced. Perhaps twenty-five per cent of Koreans are Christian and evangelists may be encountered nearly daily on street corners, in subway cars, on buses, and most certainly on television. Lee's stage direction says that the Messiah ascends to heaven, but, in the same image, the Patriotic Young Man is wearing a headband that says, "searching in the darkness."

Lee's images increase in complexity. I think it was the American poet, Archibold McCleish, who wrote that a poem does not mean — it is. *The Dummy Bride,* with all its poetic imagery on the printed page, defies simple explication, firstly because Lee Yun-Taek's production devices have a semiotics all their own and, secondly, because Lee is *not* a creator of *dramatic literature*. He is a creator of theatre events, some of which an audience may relate to an artistic whole in an intuitive way, others of which simply are baffling. A baby's crying is heard (it is the Bride's child) and the lights in the

Shindorim station glow with the birth of a new Korean mythology. The Bride and a babe are revealed, taking their place in a boat made from the Bride's stall. The area denizens throw their masks to the Bride, thus cleansing their sins. The Bride's resurrection, appearing in mourning clothing with a statue of a child, makes dramatic sense. But, why is the Blind Singer, "with a helping hand from Michael," now the owner of the white sailboat, and what are we to make of the play's ending in which all those who earlier had succumbed to bestiality are saved and the blameless Little Beggar, who cannot touch the Bride, is left alone, *un*saved, and in despair?

The Dummy Bride:
A Ceremony of Love

Dramatis Personae: (In general order of appearance.)

Blind Singer

Michael, a young beggar

Bride

Drunkard

Alienated Man #1

Jobless Young Man

Hooker

Patriotic Young Man

Alienated Man #2 *(Who becomes the Messiah, a prophet of eschatology.)*

Little Beggar

Police Sergeant

Dancing Puppet

Singing Puppet

Denizens of the Shindorim train station vicinity

SCENE 1: WHILE WAITING FOR BEAUTIFUL HUMAN BEINGS

(In front of the Shindorim Station.
The literal meaning of Shindorim is "New-City-Sylvania"
Which means "a new city built in the forest,"
implying some significant symbol.

131

Now a congested area of slums in Seoul is
established around it, with heavy traffic connecting
Seoul to the satellite cities. Kuro Industrial Complex is
near to it. It is also a hinterland of Seoul,
in which all kinds of swindles and eschatology
are rampant.[1]*)*

An opening announcement from the speakers:

"Attention, please. The train is coming to the station. Please take one step back to the line for your own safety."

(The din of a chugging passing train follows along the tracks.
A harmonica sound is heard,
"Like a bridge over troubled. . ."[2]
Enter two silhouettes against a background of twilight.
A BLIND SINGER *and* MICHAEL, *a young beggar, open the night around Shindorim Station.)*

MICHAEL: Dad!
BLIND SINGER: What?
MICHAEL: I dream every night.
BLIND SINGER: What dream?
MICHAEL: The Dummy Bride riding in a white sail boat is coming through that dark sky . . . .
BLIND SINGER: The Dummy Bride is dead.
MICHAEL: My dream isn't dead.
(The BLIND SINGER *smiles, his white, cold, hard teeth glimmering sadly. A melancholy guitar melody is heard.)*
BLIND SINGER: The Dummy Bride will not come here any more.
MICHAEL: Why?
BLIND SINGER: Because this world is a difficult place to meet those people whose lives are beautiful.
MICHAEL: *(Looking at the stars.)* This world is still beautiful. Look! The sky is filled with bright stars, so that, if I flick them with my finger *(A brief and bright intermezzo.)*, they will pour out all kind of stories.
BLIND SINGER: I can't see 'em.
MICHAEL: You lost your sight because of your dark mind.

(MICHAEL sings.)

Holding a lamplight, I would be where you are.
Holding a lamplight, the song of a bird,
I would bring water-flowing sound.
Here, on earth, under the sky,
I wait, with a lamplight,
A beautiful person.
A beautiful person.
At the end, the world is filled with danger
And that dark night-fog is our heart.
Even if the world is a doleful ocean, however,
I would be on my way to you holding a lamplight.
Holding a lamplight, I am waiting for you.
A beautiful person.[3]

(While MICHAEL*'s beautiful melody is played, the* DUMMY BRIDE
enters, pulling her pojangmacha or mobile stall, [4] *against the back-
ground of the dark sky at the Shindorim Station. Turning on a lamplight,
she takes her seat.*
The sound of a whistle in the dark.
With the whistle, a couple of Shindorim denizens enter.
The DRUNK *tosses a coin into* MICHAEL*'s can and the prelude ends.*
A LITTLE BEGGAR shouts "Dae-Han-Il-Bo-Yo"[5] *and,)*

DRUNK: Do I look like a ruffian?
   (To the audience.) Give me a break.
   Unfortunately, I take a skeptical view of this world.
   Like an old bridge over troubled water, I shake like this, though,
   In fact, I yearn to get out of this world.
   I mean, since I am sick of it, I want to be done with this world.
   I am pressed with business on all sides.
   Why doesn't the world get its teeth into me and hold me up?
   (Shaking his head.) It's over.
   It's all over!
   I will fall down.
   I am going to collapse.
   (To the audience.) Don't regret anything, you people.

   (A drunken man approaches the stall.
   He, an alienated man of our age, tries to provoke the DUMMY BRIDE
   into a senseless quarrel.)

ALIENATED MAN #1: Excuse me. Can I have a bowl of hot bean-sprouts soup?

(The DUMMY BRIDE *hands him a bowl with a smile.)*

And, uh. . . . I would like to f. . k with you just once.[6]

(The JOBLESS YOUNG MAN *standing next to him hits him in the face and glares at him with anger.)*

JOBLESS YOUNG MAN: You crazy bum. Buzz off, asshole.

(ALIENTATED MAN #1 *disappears with an injured look and the* JOBLESS YOUNG MAN *starts talking to the* DUMMY BRIDE *about the ex-world boxing champion, Hong Su-Whan, whom he encountered in the subway.)*

JOBLESS YOUNG MAN: Yesterday, I saw Hong Su-Whan at the Shin-dorim Station.
Shouting "Mommy, I've got a championship!"
That ex-boxing champion.
I felt sorry for him, though,
I've heard that his business was being liquidated.
You know what, the ex-boxing champion was standing right behind me to buy a subway ticket.
(With a smile) It was exciting, though.
He was standing right behind me.
(He's smiling again at the thought.)
(With a stiff face.) But it was very strange.
Nobody recognized Hong Su-Whan who created the legend of "4th fall, 5th success."
(Making light.) Staying in line, everybody just looked straight ahead as if to say, "Do I know you?" He is a hero who created the legend of "4th fall, 5th success."[7]
DRUNK: *(In a smart-mouthed reply.)* Legends these days are all counterfeits.

(While the JOBLESS YOUNG MAN *talks seriously, a* HOOKER *looks at the* DRUNK, *resting her chin on her hands. When the* JOBLESS YOUNG MAN *finishes talking, she starts giggling, discouraging the young man. The* DRUNK *picks a fight with the* HOOKER, *who is staring at him.)*

DRUNK: What's so funny?

HOOKER: *(Mumbling to herself.)* When I made kimchi with a couple of cabbages, I suddenly got enough energy to make my living in this world. The fact that I can make kimchi. Yes, I can make it. If I can marry somebody, so I can make kimchi with *fifty* cabbages, I would be very happy. *(Cheerfully giggling, she stares at the* DUMMY BRIDE.*)*

DRUNK: What kind of crazy bitch have we here?

(Customers in the stall are at once interested in each other's stories, but soon tire of them. A PATRIOTIC YOUNG MAN enters and distributes leaflets.)

PATRIOT: I don't know if this leaflet will start some dissension among you and be a source for fomenting distrust these days. Probably stones of criticism will be thrown from both sides. Therefore, those who receive this leaflet, please read it carefully as follows: *(Orating.)* Please read this leaflet in the manner of the petit bourgeois. It's quite all right for you to see this leaflet as an undemocratic viewpoint. It's fine with me that you are not moved, if my speech makes no sense. *(Swallowing his saliva, he talks desperately.)* We are in the midst of disaster during the so-called "great 90's."[8] The labors of patriotic young men have become meaningless. Who was it who sent the tyrant to the Baekdam temple?[9] Weren't we the very men who had the university's president's head shaved? For whom are our patriotic taxes used?

DRUNK: *(Clapping.)* Right, let's send him to the National Assembly.

PATRIOT: *(Pushing in between the people.)* Ask them what makes such a difference between our GNP and our living expenses?

DRUNK: Great! Excellent!

PATRIOT: Ask' em about some comprehensive counter-plan to cope with the increasing traffic jams.

DRUNK: You're full of shit!

PATRIOT: *(Becoming excited.)* Let's go hunt pigs fattened on our taxes!

DRUNK: I don't eat pork, bum.

PATRIOT: *(Staring and yelling at the* DRUNK.*)* Let's declare war on unjust distribution. Awake, ladies and gentlemen! You're becoming unconscious!

DRUNK: Did I inhale poison gas? Do I look like I'm out of my mind?

(The PATRIOTIC YOUNG MAN *grows angry and pulls out a canister of tear gas.)*

PATRIOT: It is the sarcasm of the petit bourgeois like you that we should guard against.

(Boom! The tear-gas canister explodes in an instant.
The stall is filled with the gas. A whistle, and
with the cries of the HOOKER *in the dark night, everyone*
scatters, with teary faces and coughing..
In the thick fog, the DUMMY BRIDE *stands alone.*
Collecting her thoughts, she peers at the world through the fog.
Carefully, her words strike the world, these words expressed
in musical scales of the first hamlet under the sky.
Sitting in the foggy world, she sings a song, "Hill of My Beloved
Land." [10]
Her song is repeated by the BLIND SINGER.)

A Song by the Blind Singer:
As time passes, I go out along the brook and the hill of my beloved land.
My soul wanders in search of home.
A small place in this world.
It's my home, and it's my hope
I will live here 'til I die.

(The HOOKER *steps forward, calling "taxi." With tottering steps, the* DRUNK, *pulls on her leg.)*

HOOKER: What the hell are you doing? You, animal!
DRUNK: An animal? Yeah, I am an animal. I am an animal indeed when May comes. Once upon a time, in May, since I was not in Gwangju, I am an animal.[11]
HOOKER: Why on earth are you treating me like this? I am Yang Shim-Suk. A man should have some conscience.
DRUNK: Conscience? What for?

(The DRUNK *gropes his hand into her skirt.*
She yells, "Ahcccck!"
Shouting, she pulls his hair with her fingers
as if plucking a chicken.
Saying "Bitch!" the DRUNK
butts her skirt with his head,
while she chops his forehead with her high-heeled shoe.

He stands up with blood running down his face and, seeing it, the
HOOKER *hides herself behind the stall counter.*
Wiping the blood off his face, the DRUNK *soliloquizes.)*

DRUNK: Yeah, it's a shame, a shame. That we are still alive is a shame.
   I would like to be reborn as an animal, this life of shame purified. As
   an animal!

   (The DRUNK *approaches the stall. The* PATRIOT *re-enters.)*

PATRIOT: Give us one more chance, please.
   Only we can save this world.
   We will do it.
   Let's go! Up to the Baegdu Mountain,
   From Halla Mountain to Baekdu Mountain.[12]

   (Denizens on the stage give him the raspberry and he is crestfallen.)

   "Home-run! It's Home-run!"

   *(ALIENATED MAN #2 of our age enters with this cheerful broadcast
   of a pro baseball game. He transforms himself into a fantastical sham
   messiah of this age.)*

MESSIAH: Yeah, although there has been no news since I ascended to
   heaven two thousand years ago, promising more than three hundred
   times in the New Testament alone that I will return, do you people
   think that you can live without me, the bridegroom of the soul? That's
   just great! You're reaping what you sowed. How dare you even think
   that you can live with confessing sins to me?
LITTLE BEGGAR: *(To the denizens.)* You don't you know what sins
   you succumb to, do you?
MESSIAH: *(Pointing at the sky strongly with his middle finger.)* The end
   is coming from the air. Since I don't want my beloved enemies living
   in sin on this soil any longer, I will cross the 38th Parallel myself, leading a large formation of Phantom bombers. I will blow up the atomic
   factory in Youngbyeon[13] first, sending our northern brothers and sis-
   ters to heaven. Then, you survivors, don't lose your chance before
   Heaven's Gate is closed!
LITTLE BEGGAR: Alleluia!
MESSIAH: Those who put on a wooden face regardless of my shouting.
   Those thoughtless people who just look out the window regardless of

the missionary pamphlets I distribute. What are you looking at out of the window? Do you see heaven there? Keep looking helplessly even when your child and wife are hunted by human traffickers.

LITTLE BEGGAR: Father!

MESSIAH: Thus far, all missing people in this city are my children. Let's go, my child. Arise! (MESSIAH *pulls the hair of the* LITTLE BEGGAR *and lifts him up to a standing position.*[14])

JOBLESS YOUNG MAN: It's a miracle, a miracle!

DRUNK: All that is just a fake.

(*The* LITTLE BEGGAR *follows* MESSIAH *and a street girl follows him, too.*

They march away with a song, "Glory, glory, halleluiah." Twirling his truncheon, a POLICE SERGEANT *watches the march of the fake* MESSIAH.)

SERGEANT: You, come over here.

MESSIAH: For what?

SERGEANT: You're a human trafficker, aren't you?

MESSIAH: Please! Would you phrase it more politely? Is saving souls for heaven trafficking in humans these days?

SERGEANT: (*Twisting his arm.*) Let's go. Our scaffold is fitter place for your kind of trash than heaven.

MESSIAH: Leave me alone! You shouldn't twist my arm like this!

SERGEANT: You son-of-a-bitch! Something about you smelled fishy, so I've followed you for the last three days and nights.

MESSIAH: O. K. Let's go.

SERGEANT: Let's move!

MESSIAH: Let's move!

SERGEANT: Move it!

MESSIAH: Move it!

SERGEANT: Move your ass, now!

MESSIAH: Hey! Hold on!

(MESSIAH *slips him some cash. Grabbing it, the* SERGEANT *puts it into his pocket, and disappears, saying, "Good-bye." An alienated man (the* MESSIAH*), the* LITTLE BEGGAR, *and a street girl exit singing the song, "A Peace Like a River to Me."*[15])

BLIND SINGER: Yes, it is.[16] Human beings began writing history because they were bored, and creating mythology lest they die alone. Jesus was crucified for alienated people, and a penniless bum, whose playground was in this factory area, now dreams about rebirth, for he is bored. Believe it or not, this is the truth. Why do I sing? Now, I can answer this question. I am alienated, therefore I sing!

(In a corner, the PATRIOT, *holding a gasoline bottle-bomb in his hand, is about to throw it, but he cannot find a place for it. He is discouraged and anxious about it. On-lookers begin to mutter.)*

DRUNK: Why the hell is that little snot playing with that bomb bottle instead of studying? He should be taken to the Samchoeng rehabilitation facility. The generation that did not experience the Korean War never understands . . . . [17]

SERGEANT: I'm with you, buddy. The world is changed. Let's get over the mutual reconciling and forgiveness and leave the past to the judgment of history. *(To the* PATRIOTIC YOUNG MAN.*)* Hey, you, come over here. Sit down here. Where do you get off, dealing out old fashioned black-and-white images of the '80's? It's no good now, you know, to chant slogans, practice resistance and dismantle the Establishment. This is an age of nostalgia. Nostalgia! If you cannot believe what I'm saying, go out and look at the expressways on Sunday. They're so jammed with the homesick that they become a giant parking lot. "Let's enjoy, let's enjoy while we are young. When you are old you can't enjoy." [18] This is our national character, isn't it? Ha, ha, ha. . . .

PATRIOT: *(Flaring up.)* Should we really live like this?

SERGEANT: What kind of scumbag is this? Eh?

JOBLESS YOUNG MAN: That's enough. You guys are going too far. *(Then the* PATRIOTIC YOUNG MAN *approaches him and hugs him.)* When the ex-boxing champ, Hong Su-Whan, defends his title out of obligation, without any press from sports writers and no guarantees, you guys are going too far.

DRUNK: What the hell are you saying about Hong Su-Whan, who now runs a billiard parlor in Incheon?

JOBLESS YOUNG MAN: The ex-world champ, Hong Su-Whan, is not a toy you play with, not something to be used once and thrown away, like a condom. He is a human being riding right next to me in the subway. Even though nobody recognized him, my meeting him . . . was beautiful. Then I confirmed that he was still putting up a good fight. [19]

(Music for "putting up a good fight" plays. . . .)

SCENE 2: A MASK PLAY OF AN AGE WITH NO PROSPECTS

(Enter a music box of the City. [20]
The fake MESSIAH'S *fantastic movable stage opens.*
Enter a singing puppet, and a dancing puppet on the movable stage.
The fake MESSIAH *delivers a sermon in the manner of a circus per-*
former doing feats of strength.)

MESSIAH: This concluding program today is a revenge play planned by
the Lord while he was nailed to the cross 1993 years ago. This is a
message of malediction planned for humankind to know the taste of
blood. Think, ladies and gentlemen! When Jesus was crucified on the
cross, what kind of feeling did he have? How painful was it? Well,
look at me! *(Stabbing himself several times, he then wipes the blood
from his body.)* This blood is truly the blood of Him when those ignorant people kicked and spat on Him. The blood of denial three times
by the learned disciple who tasted fear! *(Tears falling.)* Oh! Mary
Magdalene, my Mother. For the Lord, there was no one to trust but a
contemptuous prostitute. Those who are worse than a prostitute gov-
erned the state and learning. *(Louder to the audience.)* Who among us
helps Jesus Christ?!

DRUNK: What the hell is he doing? Splashed all over with blood . . . .

JOBLESS YOUNG MAN: That is a "Happening," so to speak. [21]

DRUNK: "Happening"?

JOBLESS YOUNG MAN: Yes. He is an *avant-garde artiste.*

PATRIOT: "Avant-garde"! Are you saying that figure is art in your eyes?
That is an image of people trying to embrace the pain of our age with
their entire being.

SERGEANT: What? Is he going to burn himself to death?

PATRIOT: *(Bursting into tears)* Yes, he is.

DRUNK: *(To the* JOBLESS YOUNG MAN.*)* What the hell have we
here? You call a man trying to burn himself to death, "avant-garde"?
Are you out of mind? *(Staring at him threateningly.)* What kind person are you?

JOBLESS YOUNG MAN: Me? I am a young pessimist of this age.

DRUNK: Because of your kind of person, this world is getting really
fucked up!

JOBLESS YOUNG MAN: *(Ashamed of himself and getting angry.)*
What's the difference between you and me? Who the hell do you think
you are?

DRUNK: Me? I am a great lower middle class citizen of the Republic of
Korea.

MESSIAH: This is the end, five minutes to go! I said the fire of judgment on this insane world would come in the form of carpet bombing!

PATRIOT: *(Interrupting.)* You're right. The age of struggle is over, and the age of the illicit union approaches. We reject the phony reconciliation . . . . . [22]

MESSIAH: Hey, hey, you! Get out of here. Do you think we want to do this shit? Dumb ass! Stay off this stage. This is our playground. We're trying to make a living here!

(The puppet play of the City begins.
The puppet in this music box moves when a coin is inserted.[23]
The DRUNK is engrossed in the singing puppet play. The JOBLESS YOUNG MAN is interested in the dancing puppet play.)

SERGEANT: Insert coin, a coin? Hah! Those are strange puppets.
(When the DRUNK inserts a coin again, "The World is Crazy"[24] plays.
Everyone on the stage dances sluggishly in a hallucinated state.
This dance looks like a scene of sodomy, while our BLIND SINGER sings. The song ends.)

BLIND SINGER: *(Speaking.)* For that woman hungering for a kiss, the theatre door is open and today again, for the lonely people, a fantastic helicopter lifts off the stage.
Women sick of routine love affairs are gathered in the theatre.
Men sick of everyday jobs are gathered in the theatre.
That woman's show is a cliché, however, the populace is already getting used to it.
An actress' posters, on which her angry-red lips are emphasized, hang on every wall in the city, and things refusing to be turned sour fall like autumn leaves.
Dear spirits, I am heading downtown. Sweet spirits, let's meet at the downtown garbage can.

(Everybody dancing to the melody from the music box disappears but the DUMMY BRIDE. She is lonely. Empty stage. Enter the PATRIOTIC YOUNG MAN. To the pathetic music, the PATRIOTIC YOUNG MAN performs a despairing suicide show. The DUMMY BRIDE keeps watch over his death. Her pure, sad requiem begins.)

BLIND SINGER: Who are you? Are you a dummy?

(She keeps silent.)

MICHAEL: Where did you come from?

DUMMY BRIDE: *(Pointing at the night sky.)* Over—there.

MICHAEL: *(Looking at the above.)* Over where?

DUMMY BRIDE: The first town under the sky.

MICHAEL: The first town under the sky? You're not supposed to be here. Here is not a good place for you to live.

DUMMY BRIDE: I will live here.

BLIND SINGER: Here things are out of joint. The world has no center.

DUMMY BRIDE: I will live here anyway. I will produce a baby, who will grow as it should be in nature. I will put my hope in my baby.

MICHAEL: It's no good for you to produce a baby. The world is being defiled by degrees, becoming a colossal dumping ground. Then, what becomes of the babies in this world? Education will be useless to them. And there would be no adults to lead them. The babies will turn out wild and crude and think only of themselves. They will be buried in a dumping ground, fighting each other.

(Exit the BLIND SINGER *and the* YOUNG BEGGAR *with the dead body of the* PATRIOTIC YOUNG MAN. *The* DUMMY BRIDE *is standing alone next to the stall. No one remains. Now, nobody comes to the stall. The* DUMMY BRIDE *disappointedly blows out the lamp. Darkness falls on the stage, and in the darkness rise murmuring masks. The* DRUNK, POLICE SERGEANT, *and the* JOBLESS YOUNG MAN *have also donned masks, and, with their bestial desires, begin their night-loitering. Everyone wears a mask and gravitates toward the stall. The* DUMMY BRIDE *happily welcomes them. It's time for people to look back with nostalgia. The* DUMMY BRIDE *cannot read their lustful desires behind the masks. They are getting drunk, talking loudly.)*

DRUNK: Over here, drinks of fire and brimstone and cyanide are ready! Friends, come over here and join us for a drink. Ha, ha, ha. . . . .

JOBLESS YOUNG MAN: Are you the one of the pretty girls? Speak up, now! How much do you charge? Don't fall in love with me. I'm wary of the selfishness called love. Let's just get it on.

SERGEANT: *(To a male on-looker who looks like an office worker.)* Are you one of the young elite of this age armed with the so-called "K. S." badge?![25] First off, get your long hair cut decently. And tighten up your necktie. *(Sarcastically.)* In this day and age, the world needs a large number of 'yes-men' like you.

JOBLESS YOUNG MAN: If anyone asked me if you have a girl friend, I would answer in a loud voice, that yeah, I got one.

DRUNK: And suppose someone persistently inquires, "Do you trust your wife?" I would say, "How about yourself?" Ha, ha, ha....

(A sodomy light is turning afar, and a drum beat sounds dolefully. The POLICE SERGEANT, the DRUNK, and the JOBLESS YOUNG MAN dance intoxicatedly in the atmosphere of the night. A mask play of an age with no prospects begins. The DUMMY BRIDE joins in the dancing, letting nature take its course. Squeaking in strange voices, the madness-soaked masks rush at the DUMMY BRIDE. What happened here? Only the DUMMY BRIDE and three masks know.)

SCENE 3: NOBODY WOULD ACCEPT THE NEW HOPE

(The DUMMY BRIDE, abandoned in the middle of the night.
A wind of this world pierces the underwear on her legs,
and her skirt becomes stained deep red as if from the crazed fuckers of this world.
She at last has a liaison with the flesh and blood of this strange world. In pain, she accepts what happened to her. The DUMMY BRIDE painfully accepts the harsh realities of her situation, robbed of her innate nature, her virginity spoiled.

Scene 3 unfolds as a slow dance of a woman who sacrifices her virginity in order to pass into an everyday life.

Enter the POLICE SERGEANT, dancing a dance of copulation.)

SERGEANT: How's business? *(With suggestively smiling eyes, he sits beside the DUMMY BRIDE.)* Hey, how 'bout a song for me?

(The DUMMY BRIDE touches his face with her out-stretched palm. She imitates a singing puppet.
The POLICE SERGEANT, with a dirty smile, takes off his police hat and touches it to her face. She grimaces once and sings.)

DUMMY BRIDE: "A night street in Hong Kong where the stars whisper. . ."[26]

(Laughing coldly in a loud voice, the POLICE SERGEANT dances a copulating dance behind her. Her song extends into the night air.

Enter the DRUNK *with tottering steps, observing their satyr-like movement.)*

DRUNK: What kind of deformed scumbag are you? *(Pointing at the* PO-LICE SERGEANT.*)* Are you human? *(Pointing to his own chest.)* The question of whether *I* live a decent life now arises. Frankly speaking, whether I am a virtuous man, I can't say for certain. Of course, though it's not my business if that scumbag screwed her or not, I feel a bit uneasy. That's why I am drinking today.

(The DRUNK *approaches the* DUMMY BRIDE *and pulls some cash out of his pocket. She chuckles with a strange look in her eyes. Taking a big breath, the* DRUNK *slips the money into her dress, and creeps under her skirt.)*

JOBLESS YOUNG MAN: *(Staring at the rocking stall.)* Great, just great! This is a stinking place with hardened shit and vicious rumors from the past. We should resolutely extract the aching tooth. *(A rotten tooth falls to the stage.[27])* If you extract the decayed tooth, a new world will arise—like a mirage. Ah—a mirage. Yes. I would like to live in it. *(The* JOBLESS YOUNG MAN *briskly approaches the "toad dancing" stall. The* BRIDE, *the* JOBLESS YOUNG MAN, *the* DRUNK, *and the* POLICE SERGEANT *perform a licentious dance of the night. The* BRIDE *gives her body freely to those three men. Then. . .)*
DUMMY BRIDE: Oh dear!
THREE MEN: What?
DUMMY BRIDE: I have a stomachache.
SERGEANT: If you have a stomachache, you should take some medicine. There are lots of good drugs these days. Go to the drug store—get'em.
DRUNK: Right, you'd better have some.
SERGEANT: *(To the* JOBLESS YOUNG MAN.*)* Hey, look! Over there, across from the Kuro Theatre, is the Ogeori Drugstore. My uncle is the pharmacist, so *(Writing something on a memo pad.)* take this and get some medicine. He'll give you a good discount. Move it.

(Crossing the stage, the JOBLESS YOUNG MAN *hurries to the drug store with the memo.The* SERGEANT *and the* DRUNK *are busy groping the* DUMMY BRIDE'S *body and exchanging goo-goo eyes. The foot-mask play[28] begins, then the* JOBLESS YOUNG MAN *rushes in with a medicine bottle.)*

JOBLESS YOUNG MAN: Hey, it's time for your medicine.

DUMMY BRIDE: *(A little tipsy.)* A glass of wine is fine with me. What's the drug for?

DRUNK: Don't prattle, please. If you wish to live in this new world, you must take it. Open up, Bride. *(The DRUNK forces her mouth open and pours the drug.*

The DUMMY BRIDE *vomits some gastric juices, and moans, holding her stomach. Stunned, everyone backs away.)*

DUMMY BRIDE: Ahhhk, bellyache. Do you think this is going to be cured with drugs?

SERGEANT: Uh? What are you talking about?

DUMMY BRIDE: This belly clearly is a pregnant one, damn you!

(POLICE SERGEANT, DRUNK and the JOBLESS YOUING MAN stare at one another, standing around her. They then put their heads together.)

SERGEANT: Whose baby is in that belly, damn it?

JOBLESS YOUNG MAN: *(Grinning.)* It's mine, probably. My father is from Jangsu Mountain,[29] you know? He said, when the red star falls in the south, a general will be born. It must be a good seed in her belly.

(A red star falls in the north.)

DRUNK: *(Looking at the night sky.)* When the red star falls in the north, what kind of baby will be born, then?

JOBLESS YOUNG MAN: *(Looking at the night sky.)* It will be a traitor.

SERGEANT: *(Looking at the sky, then at the DUMMY BRIDE.)* Then, that would be a seed of a traitor who conspires to rise in revolt against the world.

JOBLESS YOUNG MAN: No, no. The seed in that belly would not be mine. Presumably *(Giving the POLICE SERGEANT a hard time, nudges him with his foot.)*, it's yours. 'Cause your nose is bigger than mine.

SERGEANT: Well, I have a bigger nose, all right.[30] *(Sighs.)* Huh. What to do? Despite my meager salary, I already have a lover beside my wife—she *(Referring to the DUMMY BRIDE.)* would be another one? *(Throwing up his hands.)* Oh, you've got to be kidding! The seed in that belly would be *(Pointing at the* DRUNK.*)* his. The old proverb says, "The small pepper is hotter," doesn't it?

DRUNK: This guy is pulling my leg! My wife would beat me to death.

SERGEANT: Oh, me! Are you living in a world where you are beaten to death by your wife these days? I would not live with a wife who beats her husband. Come on!! You've got to be a man!

JOBLESS YOUNG MAN: Oh, shut up and try to find a way to do something!

DRUNK: If you take all responsibility for this, everything will be fine. Didn't you say that you rent a luxury officetel in the Apgujung area?[31]

JOBLESS YOUNG MAN: You said this baby will be a big trouble-maker.

SERGEANT: You get the point. We are supposed to live peacefully from now on, peacefully.

(Suddenly, the DUMMY BRIDE *stands up with grudging eyes.)*

DUMMY BRIDE: What are you guys going to do?

SERGEANT: What are you talking about?

DUMMY BRIDE: Whose baby is this?

DRUNK: How the hell should I know, damn it.

DUMMY BRIDE: Try to think again, whose baby this is!

JOBLESS YOUNG MAN: I have a no idea!

DUMMY BRIDE: *(Sighs.)* Aigo, what clumsy people you are. Ai, me . . . They say that to live a beggar's life under the bridge is better than to live as a hermit in the mountains, so I came down here, leaving my home town, the first village under the sky, where the water is clear and the people are good-hearted. Then, no man here is able to give me hope?!

SERGEANT: This lady is something! She's willing to live with three husbands?

DUMMY BRIDE: *(Clutching the* POLICE SERGEANT.*)* I don't care about myself. I can raise this baby, doing anything in this world. Please put this baby's name in your register for his sake, so he can live with a name.[32]

SERGEANT: I am a government employee! How can a government employee have a bastard?

DUMMY BRIDE: *(Clutching the* DRUNK.*)* You are an intelligent man, so this baby will not be brought up ignorant. Please take this hope which lies within my womb.

DRUNK: *(Sniveling.)* As a matter of fact, I am a learned man who can't afford *me*. My knowledge is no good for *me* to live in this world.

JOBLESS YOUNG MAN: *(Scared, he averts his eyes.)* Since I still live with my mom, under the circumstances, I can't take responsibility for it.

(The DUMMY BRIDE *turns her back to them in despair.)*

DUMMY BRIDE: *(Lamenting.)* Because they say that human beings should live together in this world, regardless of the difficulties, I descended to this lower world like a mountain brook.[33] But, this world could not accept my tiny hope.

(The DUMMY BRIDE *hops up on the bar of the stall, and hangs herself with a lamp rope.)*

SERGEANT: Hold it! *(Speaking as he goes to her.)*
DRUNK: Release that rope, now! If she dies, we're through!

(He hops up on the bar. Then the DUMMY BRIDE *slips down to the floor like autumn leaves. The rope is stretched tight.)*

JOBLESS YOUNG MAN: She's dead.

(They freeze in place. Silence for a moment.)

SERGEANT: What are we supposed to do? She wanted to kill herself!
JOBLESS YOUNG MAN: What should we do?
DRUNK: What are you talking about? Get rid of her body, so it's not seen by patrol officers.
JOBLESS YOUNG MAN: What's to worry? The police are with us.
SERGEANT: You guys have a lot of balls! What are you up to, trying to fuck me up?
DRUNK: What should we do?
SERGEANT: We should hide her body somewhere.
JOBLESS YOUNG MAN: Where? Any suggestions?
SERGEANT: Any ground! Dump her and put her in the ground. There are a lot of missing persons these days.
DRUNK: You got that right! The value of life has hit bottom these days.
JOBLESS YOUNG MAN: Let's hurry up! Move!

(As the three men approach the BRIDE*'s body, the sound of a baby crying is heard from somewhere. They are frightened and stand still for a while.)*

SERGEANT: What the hell is that noise?

JOBLESS YOUNG MAN: It's the sound of her mourning ghost.

(As they peer into the dark air, the sound of a baby crying gradually becomes clearer.)

DRUNK: It's a baby crying!

SERGEANT: What? Again? What kind of heartless bitch would throw her own baby away in the dark?[34]

(The DRUNK, with tension in his eyes, puts his ear on the BRIDE's belly.)

SERGEANT: *(Recoiling.)* What is it?

JOBLESS YOUNG MAN: *(Recoiling.)* Not a chance. It doesn't come from there, does it?

DRUNK: I'm positive it comes from here. *(Pointing at the* BRIDE's *belly.)*

SERGEANT: *(Almost crying.)* Aeeeego, what the hell's going on here!

JOBLESS YOUNG MAN: *(Excitedly.)* It's a miracle, a miracle, you guys!

SERGEANT: *(Speechless.)* Then, somebody's seed is growing in that belly, and crying now?

DRUNK: It looks that way.

(Three men are stunned. The baby crying becomes ever clearer.)

JOBLESS YOUNG MAN: *(Bursting into tears.)* Take it out immediately. How suffocating it must be!

SERGEANT: *(Bursting into tears.)* Aeeeego, geees! My baby is crying in that dead body? Aeeego, the poor thing! *(Standing up and yelling.)* Bring me a knife! I will cut her belly and take it out.

DRUNK: *(Bursting into tears.)* You can't cut out a baby whose father is unknown!

JOBLESS YOUNG MAN: What an unfeeling man you are! A man should die of old age! You mustn't leave it in in the guise of charity!

SERGEANT: You're right. Bring me a knife! Move it!

DRUNK: Hold on a second. Something about that crying is suspicious.

SERGEANT: What the hell are you talking about?

DRUNK: Don't they say that when a red star falls in the north, a traitor will be born?

JOBLESS YOUNG MAN: Turmoil in heaven and earth. If something like that really happened, he would become a great hero.

SERGEANT: Aeego, let's stay calm. I hate earth-shaking events!!

DRUNK: Let's . . . . bury it . . . . calmly.

JOBLESS YOUNG MAN: *(Yelling)* Even though you people could go on living with this burden, I am still young! I can't go on living this way. If you've come to the end of your morality, why not admit you are morally bankrupt?

(The JOBLESS YOUNG MAN *approaches the* DUMMY BRIDE.*)*

SERGEANT: *(Halts him with his truncheon.)* Don't you value your youth?

JOBLESS YOUNG MAN: What are you talking about?

DRUNK: A young pup like you should do as your elders say. These days, young people don't listen to us.

JOBLESS YOUNG MAN: *(Backing off and turning away.)* Okay, have it your way. Let's go our own ways. No problem.

SERGEANT: *(Tapping the* JOBLESS YOUNG MAN'*s shoulder.)* Hoist it up.

JOBLESS YOUNG MAN: What?

SERGEANT: *(Pointing at the* DUMMY BRIDE'*s dead body.)* Hoist it up, damn it!
(Because of the other's threatening posture, the JOBLESS YOUNG MAN *lifts the body.)* Where should we bury it?

DRUNK: *(Pointing at the Shindorim Station.)* Over there.

(The three men slowly carry the BRIDE'*s body.*
The sound of a baby's cries is drowned out by the ear-splitting din created by an arriving subway train.
It's getting dark.
The Music Box of the City comes out of the stark night.
The prophet of eschatology kneels down on the Music Box.)

MESSIAH: *(Conducting the last Mass on this planet.)* Mother, this son who could not suck thy rich milk, abundant as the sea, offers up a ton of gold cross to thee. *(Throws the cross.)* Father, this son who could not see thy resplendent aspect with side-burns like a great mountain, offers up a ton of gold shoes to thee. Oh, most dear Lord, Father, if thou art indeed a magnificent preacher, would you kindly recommend me to be an elder in Heaven? *(Pause.)* What? Do I dare dream to be an elder in Heaven after a life of such confusion? Well, if you read "dog" backwards, it reads "god," doesn't it? Now I come to thee, Father. *(Puts rope from above around his neck.)*

LITTLE BEGGAR: Sir, what are you doing over there?

MESSIAH: Well, I am looking for stars in which to be buried.

LITTLE BEGGAR: Aeego, leaving us, where are you going to go?

MESSIAH: *(Crying out to the auditorium.)* Brothers, my brothers like devils. From this day forward, when you awake, you will witness the twilight of the twentieth century.

(The MESSIAH *jumps down. Crying, the* LITTLE BEGGAR *kneels down and watches the* MESSIAH, *hanging in the air, ascend to Heaven.*

The LITTLE BEGGAR *finally lies on the ground and wails aloud.*

On another part of the stage, a study room in Heaven.

A PATRIOTIC YOUNG MAN, *reading a book closely, wears a headband on which there is a slogan: "searching in the darkness."*[35] *He grins at the* MESSIAH, *who is on his way to Heaven.*

Lights go out.

In the dark, a plaintive harmonica sound.

The BLIND SINGER *and* MICHAEL *the* YOUNG BEGGAR *appear upon the empty earth.)*

MICHAEL: *(Seeing the moving stall.)* Daddy, the lights of the stall are out! *(They approach the moving stall.)* The fire is still warm.

(This very moment, a baby's crying sound is heard again.

The crying sound grows louder, shattering the calm.

They try to find where the crying comes from.

In the great dome of the subway station

something like charcoal embers rekindles and the BLIND SINGER *and* MICHAEL *gaze at it inquiringly.*

Through them, our new mythology is regenerated, here, now.

Through these visitors, the vivid image of the bride and babe is revealed.

That image is presented as a Mother and Son statue[36] *mutually embracing, sharing body warmth. The* BLIND SINGER *and* MICHAEL *place that statue on the stall and put out the train traffic signal light of Shindorim Station.*

It is the time of dawning.

The plaza in front of the station is crowded with masked human beings.

Nothing has changed in this world, but the figures of human beings

have gradually altered into mask-like figures.
At this very moment, we hear the voice of the DUMMY BRIDE.)

VOICE OF THE BRIDE: The train is coming into the station now. For your safety, please step back to the safety line.

(The masked human beings step back and a white sail drops in front of Shindorim Station. A sailboat comes out of the dawn fog, a sailboat made of the DUMMY BRIDE's stall and, in the boat, a lamp is turned on. Now the BLIND SINGER is the owner of the white sailboat and, with a helping hand from MICHAEL, the YOUNG BEGGAR, the boat now begins a new voyage to a world with other seas of trouble. Under the sail, the bride, wearing mourning cloth, takes her seat, and, in her arms, she holds a statue of a child with open eyes.
The masked human beings begin weeping now and, removing their masks, toss them on the BRIDE's boat. They are now free of sin.
The LITTLE BEGGAR desperately follows the boat to toss his mask on to it. He catches the BRIDE's eye, and she, gazing on him, extends her hand slowly, saying,
"I will cleanse away your sins, too."
But, her hand cannot reach his mask.
The despairing figure of the LITTLE BEGGAR....)

BLACKOUT.

NOTES:

1. Shindorim is in southwestern Seoul, along the No. 2 (Green) subway line. Kuro is a short train ride away. When the play was written, these two areas were on the outskirts of Seoul, but now have been swallowed up in Seoul's rapid population boom and urban sprawl. In recent years, millions of high-rise housing units have been built as part of a government plan to reduce the severe housing shortage. There being insufficient room to build in Seoul, "new cities" by the score arise outside of Seoul, seemingly overnight.

2. From the Simon and Garfunkel 1970 hit, "Like a Bridge over Troubled Water."

3. Lee Yun-Taek revised Kim Min-Gi's song, "A Beautiful Human Being" (1972), to fit his dramatic purpose here. The last stanza of Kim's lyrics is this: In a dazzling white snowfall/Standing tall and alone on a mountain/When a song sounds/In that gentle soul/Mm. . ./That beautiful one/Is a human being/A beautiful human being.

4. The Korean *pojangmacha* (*pojang*=pavement, *macha*=horse cart) is an ubiquitous mobile vending cart found on the streets of Seoul, around which the customers

may stand or perch on stools to eat. Some of the fancier carts provide tables and chairs under make-shift awnings. Stalls specialize in various kinds of snacks or late-night meals. Some are popular with students on the way to after-school tutorial classes and others are favored by people of the night in search of warm, cheap food and warming, cheap clear liquor (*soju*).The stalls often are left in place for days when business is good, then moved by human power, not by horses, to another location as necessary.

5. The *Daehan Ilbo* (Korean Daily News) is a newspaper being sold by the Beggar.

6. The Korean text suggests "do it with you" or some intimation close to that. But the line is not vocalized. The actor will need to suggest the lewd undertone of the line.

7. Hong Su-Hwan was knocked down four times in a 1977 bout with Hector Carrasquilla before he scored a knockout to win the WBA's junior featherweight championship. Out of his feat arose the saying, *sajeon-ogi*: "Knocked down four times, but rising up five times." For other variations on the theme of endurance, see Sang-Hun Choe and Christopher Torchia, *How Koreans Talk: A Collection of Expressions* (Seoul: Unhaeng-Namu, 2002).

8. During the 1990s, South Korea emerged as a "Little Tiger," an economic power in Asia. Standards of living soared but the nation paid a price in degraded environment, diminished traditional values, and reliance on the United States as a trading partner and U.S. armed forces stationed South Korea.

9. The "tyrant" referred to is Chun Doo-Hwan (1931-), President of South Korea 1980–88, during whose ruthless presidency a student, Park Jong-Cheol, was suffocated to death during a police interrogation. Unrest ensued and crack troops were sent against civilians in the infamous "Gwangju Incident," May 17–27, 1980, in which hundreds of civilians were killed. The Baegdam (Baek-Tam) temple is located in the Seorak Mountain area in the northeast corner of South Korea. Chun Doo-Whan was exiled there following his reign as president. As for the head shaving, a university president may in fact have been forced by students to shave his head, an act of utter humiliation.

10. A Korean folk song popular among those away from their home towns.

11. The Drunk likely refers to the fact that he did not join the ranks of civilians who fought crack government troops during the "Gwangju Incident" May 17–27, 1980. The event seems to remain an unhealed wound in the South Korean national psyche.

12. Halla Mountain (written on maps as *Hallasan*) is a mythically important site that dominates the middle of Jejudo (Cheju Island) at the southern tip of the Korean peninsula. Baekdu Mountain (frequently written as *Paekdusan*), also is a mountain with ancient mythical power in Korean history and culture. It is the highest mountain in Korea, situated in North Korea on the 42nd Parallel. The Patriot seems to be suggesting that the citizens from the southern tip to the northern extreme of Korea should rise up against oppression.

13. Yeongbyeon (*Yŏngbyŏn*) lies north of the North Korean capital, along the Cheongcheon River (*Ch'ŏngch'ŏng*).

14. The Little Beggar up to this point has been faking legs that would not support him—or having no legs at all. Thus, when he "stands," it is a "miracle."

15. "Thus says the Lord, your Redeemer, the Holy One of Israel: 'I am the Lord your God, who teaches you for your profit, who leads you in the way you should go. Oh, that you had listened to my commandments; then your peace would be like a river and your rightcousness like the waves of the sea. . .'" Isaiah 48: 17–18 "Peace Like a River" is a well-known spiritual. About twenty-five per cent of Koreans are Christian, so references to the Bible and Christian hymns are not as strange as they might appear.

16. The response is to the Drunk's, "All that is just a fake."

17. The Samcheong facility is a place for the enforced "rehabilitation" of mobsters and members of the political opposition. In the Korean text, the Drunk actually refers only to the beginning of the Korean Conflict, June 26, 1950, but, by extension refers to the entire conflict, 1950–53. His sentiments also the gap between younger and older generations, most especially in regard to unification of the North and South and the continuing presence of 37,000 U.S. troops on South Korean soil. The Drunk suggests that the Patriotic Young Man should be in the military. By law, Korean men must spend twenty-six months in the military or other acceptable forms of civil service.

18. From a Korean folk song about "seizing the day," the title of which means "Sleeping Around during Youth." This same song used in *O-Gu*.

19. Koreans shout *"hwaiting"* ("fighting") to cheer on their team, to give support to students studying for major exams, to urge on more toasts at drinking parties. The term received world-wide recognition during the Korean soccer team's rise to prominence in the Seoul-hosted World Cup.

20. The "music box" is a moving mechanical stage device, on and around which actors move or dance.

21. A term for a performance 'event' that gained popularity in the West in the 1960s, in which chance occurrences and improvisation were features and audience participation encouraged. See, for example, Oscar Brockett, *History of the Theatre*, 8th ed. (Boston: Allyn and Bacon, 1999), 582.

22. The "illicit union" and the "phony reconciliation" refer to the much-discussed reunification of North and South Korea. Although the politically necessary stance in South Korea is pro-reunification, there seems to be an increasing understanding of the costs of reunification, most especially the overwhelming economic cost and its negative impact on the South Korea standard of living. However, because millions of Koreans in the North and South remain separated from their families, reunification is an emotional issue in the lives of many South Koreans, nearly sixty years after the establishment of the two nations.

23. The puppet is in fact an actor; the "slot" for the coin is the actor/puppet's mouth.

24. South Korean song popular during the 1980s. The literal title, in English, is "The World is a Kaleidoscope" or "Kaleidoscope of Life." Some of the lyrics are as follows: "The world is a kaleidoscope, a kaleidoscope of life./Handsome ones are having sweet lives, ugly ones are having hard lives./yai-yai-ya, listen to me, please./Here there are fake lives, there are fake lives./Fake lives are everywhere."

25. The "K.S. badge" refers to elite status coming from attending the best schools. "K" stands for South Korea's best prep school and "S" stands for Seoul National University, the nation's most prestigious university.

26. A popular song at the time. In English, "A Girl of Hong Kong." There is a slang phrase in Korean, *Hong Kong ganda* ("I'm going to Hong Kong.") which has come to mean "I am in heaven."

27. The tooth is an example of Lee Yun-Taek's theatrical imagination, unconventional and unpredictable. The script is built of dream-like or fantastic vignettes; thus, the tooth is consistent with the theatrical world Lee has created.

28. A "foot-mask" play (*Baltal*) is a traditional Korean puppet form in which the mask is worn on the feet to create the head, with strings or rods sometimes connected to long-sleeved puppet arms. The feet are inserted through a curtain behind which the puppeteer may recline or lay on his side. Accompanied by wind and percussion instruments, the wise-cracking entertainment satirizes the corrupt upper class and frankly encapsulates the joys and sorrows of the lower class in earlier days. Though the form has been designated Important Intangible Cultural Property No. 79 by the Korean government, its popularity has waned in the face of electronic entertainment. However, Lee Yun-Taek, along with a few other modern theatre writers and directors, such as Oh Tae-Sŏk and Sohn Jinchaek, has been instrumental in using traditional theatre forms and music to create modern works with a clearly Korean artistic sensitivity.

29. The Chinese characters," jang" and "su," combine to mean "live a long life."

30. As one may surmise, they are discussing anatomy other than noses. The Sergeant's later reference to "smaller peppers being hotter" suggests that the Drunk is short of stature, but has an allusion to red peppers being hung outside a home in which there is a newborn baby boy.

31. Apgujung is a trendy area in Seoul, in the newer area south of the Han River that runs through the city. It is referred to as "Seoul's Rodeo Drive," a place where style is prized and lots of money is a seeming necessity. It is doubtful that the Jobless Man could afford an "officetel" in the area. The reader must decide if the Drunk is being sarcastic or not.

32. Family life is central to Korean culture and family registration books trace lineage back for generations. A child without a traceable ancestry is at best disadvantaged, at worst a non-person.

33. That is, pure and gaily, a bringer of life.

34. The Sergeant does not yet understand that the sound is not that of a baby abandoned nearby, but that of the baby in the Bride's womb.

35. Four Korean or Chinese syllables are used for the headband: Am-Jung-Mo-Saek.

36. The Western world's "Madonna and Child" or the "Pieta" are appropriate parallel images here.

Selected Bibliography

Listed here are only those works that were most useful in the translation of the plays and the writing of introductory sections. There is a good deal of information about modern Korean theatre and Lee Yun-Taek available in Korean-language editions, but criticism of Lee's plays and translations of his theoretical writings are not available in English-language editions.

Eckert, Carter J., Ki-baik Lee, Lew Young-Ick, Michael Robinson, Edward W. Wagner. *Korea Old and New: A History*. Seoul: Ilchokak Publishers, 1990.

Choe, Sang-Hun and Christopher Torchia. *How Koreans Talk: A Collection of Expressions*. Seoul: Eunhaeng Namu Publishing, 2002.

Chung, Jin-soo. "Korean Theatre, Past and Present." *Korea Journal* 20 (March 1980): 4–9.

Han, Sang-chul. "Trends in Postwar Theatre." *Korean Cultural Heritage*. Vol. 3, *Performing Arts*. ed. Korea Foundation. Seoul: Samsung Moonwha Printing, 1997, 196–206.

Jang, Won-Jae. *Irish Influences on Korean Theatre during the 1920s and 1930s*, Buckinghamshire, UK: Colin Smythe Limited, 2003.

Kim, Ah-Jeong. "The Modern Uses of Tradition in Contemporary Korean Theatre—A Critical Analysis from an Intercultural Perspective." PhD diss., University of Illinois, 1995.

Kim, Ah-jeong and R.B. Graves, trans. *The Metacultural Theatre of Oh T'ae-sŏk: Five Plays from the Korean Avant-Garde*. Honolulu: University of Hawai'i Press, 1999.

Kim, Ho-Soon. "The Development of Modern Korean Theatre in South Korea." PhD diss., University of Kansas, 1974.

Kim, Hyunggyu. *Understanding Korean Literature*. Translated by Robert J. Fouser. Armonk, NY: M.E. Sharpe, 1997.

Kim, Jinhee. "Disembodying the Other: East-West Relations and Modern Korean Drama." PhD diss., Indiana University 1996.

Kim, Moon-hwan. "Ideology and Historical Influences in Modern Drama." Pp. 224–231 in *Korean Cultural Heritage*. Vol. 3, *Performing Arts*, ed. Korea Foundation. Seoul: Samsung Moonwha Printing, 1997.

Kim, Yun-cheol. "Theatre in the 1990s." *Koreana* 11 (Summer, 1997): 32–35.

———. "The Influence of Western Drama on Contemporary Korean Theatre." *European Cultural Review.* <http://www.c3.hu/~eufuzetek/en/eng/15/index.php?=yuncheol> (Dec. 2005).

———. *Uri neun Jikum Juhak ui Shidaero Kaneun ga?* (Where is Our Current Banal Criticism Headed?). Seoul: Yeongeuk-kwa In-gan Publishers, 2000.

Kim, Yun-Cheol, and Miy-Ye Kim, eds. *Contemporary Korean Theatre: Playwrights, Directors, Stage-Designers*. Seoul: Theatre and Man Press, 2000.

Koo, Hee-sue. "Major Theatrical Groups." *Koreana* 11 (Summer, 1997): 22–31.

Koo, John H. and Andrew C. Nahm, eds. *An Introduction to Korean Culture*. Elizabeth, NJ: Hollym International Corp., 1997.

Korean International Theatre Institute, ed. *Korean Performing Arts: Drama, Dance and Music Theatre*. Seoul: Jipmoondang Publishing, 1997.

Lee, Meewon. "Korean Modern Theatre Seeking for its National and Cultural Identity." < http://www.twscholl.net/ASTR/Docs/ASTR%20Lee.doc > (Sept. 2005).

Lee, Yun-Taek. *Laugh, Beat Drum, Die* [Utta, Bukchida, Jukda]. Seoul: Yeongmin-sa Publishers, 1997.

National Academy of the Korean Language. *An Illustrated Guide to Korean Culture*. Seoul: Hakgojae Publishing Co., 2002.

"Performing Arts Venues." *Koreana* 11 (Summer 1997): 36–43.

Pratt, Keith and Richard Rutt. *Korea: A Historical and Cultural Dictionary*. Surrey, UK: Curzon Press, 1999.

Shim, Jung Soon. "In Search of Diversity: Korean Theatre in the 1980s." *Korean Culture* (Fall 1991): 5–9.

Soh, Yon-Ho. "Ritual Reborn in Modern Theatre." Pp. 216–223 in *Korean Cultural Heritage*. Vol. 3, *Performing Arts*, ed. Korea Foundation. Seoul: Samsung Moonwha Printing, 1997.

Song, Ki-joong. *Glossary of Korean Culture*. Seoul: Jimoon-dang Publishers, 2001.

Suh, Yon-Ho. "Status and Prospects of Korean Political Drama." *Korea Journal* 28 (August 1989): 19–30.